# Managing Quality in Qualitative Research

*Managing Quality in Qualitative Research* (by Uwe Flick) is the eight part of *The SAGE Qualitative Research Kit*. This *Kit* comprises eight books and taken together the *Kit* represents the most extensive and detailed introduction to the process of doing qualitative research. This book can be used in conjunction with other titles in the *Kit* as part of this overall introduction to qualitative methods but this book can equally well be used on its own as an introduction to the management of quality in qualitative research.

### Complete list of titles in *The SAGE Qualitative Research Kit*

- Designing Qualitative Research *Uwe Flick*
- Doing Interviews *Steinar Kvale*
- Doing Ethnographic and Observational Research *Michael Angrosino*
- Doing Focus Groups *Rosaline Barbour*
- Using Visual Data in Qualitative Research *Marcus Banks*
- Analyzing Qualitative Data *Graham R. Gibbs*
- Doing Conversation, Discourse and Document Analysis *Tim Rapley*
- Managing Quality in Qualitative Research *Uwe Flick*

### Members of the Editorial Advisory Board

# Managing Quality in Qualitative Research

## Uwe Flick

Los Angeles • London • New Delhi • Singapore

H62
.F55
2007x

H62
.S28
2007x
[vol. 8]

SAGE Publications Ltd
1 Oliver's Yard
55 City Road
London EC1Y 1SP

SAGE Publications Inc.
2455 Teller Road
Thousand Oaks, California 91320

SAGE Publications India Pvt Ltd
B 1/I 1 Mohan Cooperative Industrial Area
Mathura Road, New Delhi 110 044
India

SAGE Publications Asia-Pacific Pte Ltd
33 Pekin Street #02-01
Far East Square
Singapore 048763

**Library of Congress Control Number 2006938290**

**British Library Cataloguing in Publication data**

A catalogue record for this book is available from the British Library

ISBN 978-0-7619-4982-4

Typeset by C&M Digitals (P) Ltd, Chennai, India
Printed in Great Britain by The Cromwell Press Ltd, Trowbridge, Wiltshire
Printed on paper from sustainable resources

# ▓ Contents

# III List of illustrations

## Boxes

## Figures

## Tables

# Editorial introduction
## Uwe Flick

- An introduction to *The SAGE Qualitative Research Kit*
- What is qualitative research?
- How do we conduct qualitative research?
- Scope of *The SAGE Qualitative Research Kit*

## Introduction to *The SAGE Qualitative Research Kit*

In recent years, qualitative research has enjoyed a period of unprecedented growth and diversification as it has become an established and respected research approach across a variety of disciplines and contexts. An increasing number of students, teachers and practitioners are facing questions and problems of how to do qualitative research – in general and for their specific individual purposes. To answer these questions, and to address such practical problems on a how-to-do level, is the main purpose of *The SAGE Qualitative Research Kit*.

The books in *The SAGE Qualitative Research Kit* collectively address the core issues that arise when we actually do qualitative research. Each book focuses on key methods (e.g. interviews or focus groups) or materials (e.g. visual data or discourse) that are used for studying the social world in qualitative terms. Moreover, the books in the Kit have been written with the needs of many different types of reader in mind. As such, the Kit and the individual books will be of use to a wide variety of users:

- *Practitioners* of qualitative research in the social sciences, medical research, marketing research, evaluation, organizational, business and management studies, cognitive science, etc., who face the problem of planning and conducting a specific study using qualitative methods.
- *University teachers* and lecturers in these fields using qualitative methods will be expected to use these series as a basis of their teaching.

- *Undergraduate and graduate students* of social sciences, nursing, education, psychology and other fields where qualitative methods are a (main) part of the university training including practical applications (e.g. for writing a thesis).

Each book in *The SAGE Qualitative Research Kit* has been written by a distinguished author with extensive experience in their field and in the practice with methods they write about. When reading the whole series of books from the beginning to the end, you will repeatedly come across some issues which are central to any sort of qualitative research – such as ethics, designing research or assessing quality. However, in each book such issues are addressed from the specific methodological angle of the authors and the approach they describe. Thus you may find different approaches to issues of quality or different suggestions of how to analyze qualitative data in the different books, which will combine to present a comprehensive picture of the field as a whole.

## What is qualitative research?

It has become more and more difficult to find a common definition of qualitative research which is accepted by the majority of qualitative research approaches and researchers. Qualitative research is no longer just simply '*not quantitative research*', but has developed an identity (or maybe multiple identities) of its own.

Despite the multiplicity of approaches to qualitative research, some common features of qualitative research can be identified. Qualitative research is intended to approach the world 'out there' (not in specialized research settings such as laboratories) and to understand, describe and sometimes explain social phenomena 'from the inside' in a number of different ways:

- By analyzing experiences of individuals or groups. Experiences can be related to biographical life histories or to (everyday or professional) practices; they may be addressed by analyzing everyday knowledge, accounts and stories.
- By analyzing interactions and communications in the making. This can be based on observing or recording practices of interacting and communicating and analyzing this material.
- By analyzing documents (texts, images, film or music) or similar traces of experiences or interactions.

Common to such approaches is that they seek to unpick how people construct the world around them, what they are doing or what is happening to them in terms that are meaningful and that offer rich insight. Interactions and documents are seen as ways of constituting social processes and artefacts collaboratively (or conflictingly). All of these approaches represent ways of meaning, which can be reconstructed and analyzed with different qualitative methods that allow the researcher to develop (more or less generalizable) models, typologies, theories as ways of describing and explaining social (or psychological) issues.

## How do we conduct qualitative research?

Can we identify common ways of doing qualitative research if we take into account that there are different theoretical, epistemological and methodological approaches to qualitative research and that the issues that are studied are very diverse as well? We can at least identify some common features of how qualitative research is done.

- Qualitative researchers are interested in accessing experiences, interactions and documents in their natural context and in a way that gives room to the particularities of them and the materials in which they are studied.
- Qualitative research refrains from setting up a well-defined concept of what is studied and from formulating hypotheses in the beginning in order to test them. Rather, concepts (or hypotheses, if they are used) are developed and refined in the process of research.
- Qualitative research starts from the idea that methods and theories should be appropriate to what is studied. If the existing methods do not fit to a concrete issue or field, they are adapted or new methods or approaches are developed.
- Researchers themselves are an important part of the research process, either in terms of their own personal presence as researchers, or in terms of their experiences in the field and with the reflexivity they bring to the role – as are members of the field under study.
- Qualitative research takes context and cases seriously for understanding an issue under study. A lot of qualitative research is based on case studies or a series of case studies, and often the case (its history and complexity) is an important context for understanding what is studied.
- A major part of qualitative research is based on text and writing – from field notes and transcripts to descriptions and interpretations and finally to the presentation of the findings and of the research as a whole. Therefore, issues of transforming complex social situations (or other materials such as images) into texts – issues of transcribing and writing in general – are major concerns of qualitative research.
- If methods are supposed to be adequate to what is under study, approaches to defining and assessing the quality of qualitative research (still) have to be discussed in specific ways that are appropriate for qualitative research and even for specific approaches in qualitative research.

# The Scope of *The SAGE Qualitative Research Kit*

- *Designing Qualitative Research* (Uwe Flick) gives a brief introduction to qualitative research from the point of view of how to plan and design a concrete study using qualitative research in one way or the other. It is intended to outline a framework for the other books in *The Sage Qualitative Research Kit* by focusing on how-to-do problems and on how to solve such problems in the research process. The book will address issues of constructing a research design in qualitative research; it will outline stepping stones in making a research project work and will discuss practical problems such as resources in qualitative research but also more methodological issues like quality of qualitative research and also ethics. This framework is spelled out in more details in the other books in the Kit.
- Three books are devoted to collecting or producing data in qualitative research. They take up the issues briefly outlined in the first book and approach them in a much more detailed and focused way for the specific method. First, *Doing Interviews* (Steinar Kvale) addresses the theoretical, epistemological, ethical and practical issues of interviewing people about specific issues or their life history. *Doing Ethnographic and Observational Research* (Michael Angrosino) focuses on the second major approach to collecting and producing qualitative data. Here again practical issues (like selecting sites, methods of collecting data in ethnography, special problems of analyzing them) are discussed in the context of more general issues (ethics, representations, quality and adequacy of ethnography as an approach). In *Doing Focus Groups* (Rosaline Barbour) the third of the most important qualitative methods of producing data is presented. Here again we find a strong focus on how-to-do issues of sampling, designing and analyzing the data and on how to produce them in focus groups.
- Three further volumes are devoted to analyzing specific types of qualitative data. *Using Visual Data in Qualitative Research* (Marcus Banks) extends the focus to the third type of qualitative data (beyond verbal data coming from interviews and focus groups and observational data). The use of visual data has not only become a major trend in social research in general, but confronts researchers with new practical problems in using them and analyzing them and produces new ethical issues. In *Analyzing Qualitative Data* (Graham Gibbs), several practical approaches and issues of making sense of any sort of qualitative data are addressed. Special attention is paid to practices of coding, of comparing and of using computer-assisted qualitative data analysis. Here, the focus is on verbal data like interviews, focus groups or biographies. *Doing Conversation, Discourse and Document Analysis* (Tim Rapley) extends this focus to different types of data, relevant for analyzing discourses. Here, the focus is on existing material (like documents) and on recording everyday

conversations and on finding traces of discourses. Practical issues such as generating an archive, transcribing video materials and of how to analyze discourses with such types of data are discussed.

- *Managing the Quality of Qualitative Research* (Uwe Flick) takes up the issue of quality in qualitative research, which has been briefly addressed in specific contexts in other books in the Kit, in a more general way. Here, quality is looked at from the angle of using or reformulating existing or defining new criteria for qualitative research. This book will examine the ongoing debates about what should count as defining 'quality' and validity in qualitative methodologies and will examine the many strategies for promoting and managing quality in qualitative research. Special attention is paid to the strategy of triangulation in qualitative research and to the use of quantitative research in the context of promoting the quality of qualitative research.

Before I go on to outline the focus of this book and its role in the Kit, I would like to thank some people at Sage who were important in making this Kit happen: Michael Carmichael suggested this project to me some time ago and was very helpful with his suggestions in the beginning. Patrick Brindle took over and continued this support, as did Vanessa Harwood and Jeremy Toynbee in making books out of the manuscripts we provided.

# About this book
## Uwe Flick

The problem of how to address the issue of quality in qualitative research has been taken up at several points in the other books in *The SAGE Qualitative Research Kit*. It is still a crucial problem in qualitative research in general, for which it has to find solutions and answers. The authors of the other books have turned to this issue at the same time more generally and more specifically than is the focus of this book. They were more specific, as they discuss problems of quality or validity for one specific approach – the method they discuss in their book. So Kvale (2007) has given instructive reflections about the validity and objectivity of interview research, Angrosino (2007) does the same for observation and ethnography and Barbour (2007) for using focus groups. That is why they are more specific than this book.

On the other hand, this book is more specific than the other ones in *The SAGE Qualitative Research Kit* in this respect, as it tries to outline concrete strategies of how to manage the problem of quality in qualitative research. In this context, it tries not to reduce the whole problem to an issue linked to the (correct or reflexive) use of one specific method or step in the research process. Rather one focus of this book is to take the research process as a whole as a starting point for addressing issues of quality in qualitative research. Thus it is oriented on quality management and transparency of the research process as one way of addressing quality issues. The second focus is on extending the usual way of conceptualizing the research process, and the book makes several suggestions for that. Strategies of managing diversity aim at extending the research to examples that do not directly fit into the finding or into what is expected. Strategies of triangulation extend the research at several points – by integrating an additional theoretical or personal perspective, by using more than one methodological approach, and so on.

In general, the book discusses answers to quality issues in several ways: by using or (re-)formulating quality criteria and by developing and applying strategies of quality promotion and management. In this sense, the book has two functions in the context of *The SAGE Qualitative Research Kit*: as a stand-alone book it aims at giving a comprehensive account of the problems and solutions in the field of managing quality in qualitative research; as an addition to the other books in the *Kit*, it rounds up the framework for the other books at a methodological level.

# 1
# How to address research quality

**Chapter objectives**
After reading this chapter, you should

- see the relevance of the issue of quality for the further development and establishment of qualitative research;
- have an impression of the angles and levels at which this issue becomes relevant; and
- have an overview of the following chapters and of how they address the issue.

## The relevance of quality issues in qualitative research

Qualitative research has come of age. The growing number of textbooks, journals, other publications and the extension of research practice across several disciplines demonstrate this. Perhaps another indicator for this development or a need resulting from it is the current relevance of the question of how to evaluate qualitative research, the plans, the methods and the results obtained with them. The phase of development in which researchers simply trust their methods according to what Glaser suggests: 'Trust grounded theory, it works, just do it, use it and publish!' (1998, p. 254), seems to be over. Instead of such (maybe somewhat naïve) optimism, we now find many articles devoted to criteria, to checklists, to standards, to quality, to rigour and evaluation of qualitative research.

In contrast to earlier stages in the development of qualitative research, questions about the quality of qualitative research are no longer raised mainly to demonstrate (from outside) that there is a lack of scientific quality in qualitative research. Rather this question is increasingly raised from the inside with a 'how to' perspective: how to assess or evaluate what we are doing, how to demonstrate quality in qualitative research in an active and self-confident way. How to manage the issue of quality in the qualitative research process has become a topic of major relevance for the further development of qualitative research as a whole. Today it is less the acceptance of qualitative research as such (compared to quantitative research, for example) but the acceptance of specific procedures and results in a single piece of research (for reasons of funding or of publication, for example) that is at stake. Thus, the focus of the discussion about quality of qualitative research has – not completely, but mainly – shifted from fundamental, epistemological and philosophical levels to more concrete and practical levels of research.

## Internal needs and external challenges

Nevertheless, discussions about the quality of qualitative research are located at the crossroads of internal needs and external challenges. The internal needs arise from the development and proliferation of qualitative research as a field. We find more and more alternatives of how to do qualitative research, a growing variety of methodological alternatives and epistemological and conceptual programs. Qualitative research can no longer be associated with one or two specific methods. Rather, we find different research programs with different backgrounds, intentions and strategies of how to do research. Although we can identify common features of qualitative research across the different programs (see Flick, 2006a, chaps 2 and 6, or Flick et al., 2004a, for suggestions), we can see these programs in an internal competition. Thus, we can address issues of quality of qualitative research inside the single research program: What is good grounded theory research (see Gibbs, 2007)? What makes it distinct from bad examples? We can also address these issues inside qualitative research from a comparative perspective: What makes a specific grounded theory study a good example of qualitative research? What makes it more appropriate than a discourse analysis (see Rapley, 2007) about the same topic? In both cases, the issue of quality is raised from inside qualitative research and inside qualitative research practice, and thus internally.

External challenges to qualitative research linked with these issues become relevant, once qualitative research becomes competitive with other approaches of research. This is the case when qualitative research wants to enter fields traditionally dominated by other forms of research. When qualitative researchers in psychology, for example, want to publish their research in peer-reviewed journals, which were traditionally experimentally oriented, the need to demonstrate that the single piece of research is a good example becomes a challenge. Or when, for example, medical sociologists want to publish a study using qualitative methods in a medical journal, where not only other disciplines but also the ideals of natural science are dominant, the quality issue becomes even more relevant.

Another field of competition is funding of research in areas in which traditionally experimental or quantitative researchers are dominant. Here again, issues of quality are raised from outside to assess the single grant application, to compare it with grant applications from other backgrounds, or simply to have good arguments to reject proposals.

And finally, teaching and curriculum planning has become a field where qualitative research is in competition with other approaches for resources: what is the part of qualitative research in the curriculum for psychologists or sociologists, and what is the relation to more quantitative or experimental approaches?

In all these fields, the ability of qualitative research to demonstrate that there are criteria, strategies and approaches to distinguish good from bad research and to enhance and reassure the quality of qualitative research is an external challenge. The better qualitative researchers are able to present solutions to this problem, the more successful will they be in establishing themselves in these fields against competitors. As we will see later in this book, the issue of quality in qualitative research is not only a technical problem but also refers to the quality of results and insights from the research, or the study (what's new in it?).

## Four levels of asking the question of quality

Following from what has been said so far, the question of quality in (qualitative) research can be asked at four different levels and by four different groups of actors.

### The researcher's interests in knowing about how good or bad their own research is

Novices to research in particular will have an interest in judging how far they can trust their results and whether they applied their methods in a correct way – and more generally how good their own research is. How can I find out whether the interview I did is a good interview (see Kvale, 2007)? How can I find out how far I can trust my findings from this or from my other interviews? And finally, what conclusions can I draw from them in a well-founded way? How can I be sure that insights from these interviews represent what the interviewee thinks or experienced? If I work with other researchers, how can we be sure that each of us proceeds in a similar way, so that the interviews and results are comparable at the level of the interviewees and not only at the level of the differences in the interviewers' behaviour? In this context, quality criteria or strategies to assess and improve the quality of research will be seen as helpful to reassure oneself and

3

to prepare for the evaluation and critique by others (doctoral committees, for example). But also questions of originality and novelty might puzzle the researchers concerning their study.

## Funding institutions' interest in evaluating what should be or has been granted

The issue of evaluation becomes relevant in the process of funding research at two points. First of all, a proposal has to be evaluated for its consistency and adequacy for what is to be studied and for the quality of the results that can be expected. Second, at the end of the funding, the research or the report has to be evaluated for which of the promises have been kept, how well the research was planned and carried out according to the plan, and in general what came out of the whole study. Here again, comparability becomes a relevant issue: how is the single (qualitative) proposal comparable with other qualitative proposals and how can it be compared with proposals coming from other disciplines such as natural or technology sciences? Review processes often pass several levels of committees before a final decision is taken and are mostly based on reviews from several scientists. Qualitative research, with its flexibility and openness in how the research is planned and practised, is often less compatible with such review processes than standardized or experimental research, where the planning is mostly done at the outset of the process.

These are reasons why considerable input to the internal discussion about how to assess the quality of qualitative research has recently come from funding institutions like the ESRC in the UK, the National Institutes of Health in the US or the German Research Council. Their input was to ask researchers from different qualitative traditions to set up lists of criteria and checklists allowing them to make judgements and decisions more rational and transparent (see Chapter 2). The results from such activities have led to a renewed intensification of the academic discussion about quality issues, as many researchers do not see their special approach or qualitative research in general represented in such (check-)lists.

## Journal editors' interest in deciding what to publish and what not

A similar trend can be observed in the context of publishing qualitative research. The more the number of peer-reviewed journal articles becomes a general indicator for the scientific quality and merits of single researchers, research groups, institutes, faculties and even universities, the more qualitative research has to be submitted and peer reviewed also. Here again, we see the problem of how to make this process rational and transparent for those who submit a paper or are asked for reviews of qualitative papers. Again, we find attempts to set up checklists to evaluate the research that is reported and at the same time to evaluate the way in which the research is reported and made transparent. Here, the quality issue is in some way doubled. Consideration of rigour and criteria in the research is seen as essential if the research is to be published. The research in its presentation has to be linked back to existing literature, for example – which is a criterion at the level of presentation.

### Readers' interest in orientation of which research to rely on and which not

This brings us to the fourth level, at which the quality issue becomes relevant. If you read an article about a study with interesting findings, you might like to know how far these findings are based on what was studied and what allows you to trust what you read. This is the more general description of the relevance of the quality issue on the side of the user of qualitative research. In standardized research, reliability, validity and significance tests also have the function of allowing a rather simple and fast credibility check about the study and its results. This will not be transferable to qualitative research (see Chapter 2), but criteria or checklists might be the way to answer the question of credibility. In any case, it would be helpful for the reception of qualitative research if a comparable 'instrument' were available and generally accepted here.

## The problem: how to assess the quality of qualitative research

So far, I have outlined the relevance of taking up the quality issue in the discussion of qualitative research. In what follows, I will focus more on what the general problems of establishing instruments of quality assurance in qualitative research are like. These problems might be the reason why – unlike quantitative research – a general canon of criteria has so far not been established and accepted in qualitative research.

### Research evaluation based on standardization?

In quantitative and experimental research, we find a close link between evaluation of research and the standardization of research situations. In order to increase the internal and external validity of research and results, interfering conditions are controlled. If the interrelation of two variables is to be tested, the exclusion of interfering variables is a way to guarantee the internal validity of the interrelation that was measured. The exclusion of interfering variables can best be achieved by standardizing the research situation so that no uncontrolled influences may interfere. That is why psychological research ended up mainly in the experimental laboratory, where the chances of having such a control are high. External

5

validity means the generalization of results from the research situation (and case) to other situations and cases. Again, excluding interfering variables, for example biases in sampling, warrants this. Therefore, random sampling is applied in quantitative research, because it allows for excluding any biases in the sample. Similar examples could be given for the case of reliability (see also Chapter 2). What these examples show is that in quantitative and experimental research, criteria like validity and reliability are conceptualized in ways that rely heavily on standardization of the research situation. If these criteria and these conceptualizations are applied to qualitative research, they are confronted with research situations that profit greatly from not being standardized, from not being located in laboratories and from not being characterized by a similar degree of control.

What does this mean for our context? If research evaluation is strongly linked to standardization of research situations and practices, traditional ways of evaluating research are difficult to use in qualitative research, although the main intention of research evaluation may still be relevant. If we take the everyday meaning of the words, qualitative researchers too are interested to know whether (their) results are 'valid' and whether they can 'rely' on them. But that interest does not necessarily mean that they adopt the procedures and conditions of the ways validity and reliability are checked in standardized research. As it seems, there is a need to ask such questions but also a need to develop adequate ways of answering them. This is the first dimension of the problem – a need to ask similar questions but also a need to develop appropriate ways of answering them. But what has been said so far makes it rather unlikely that qualitative research will fit into the concept of general criteria for all sorts of empirical (social) research or general solutions to the quality issue for all sciences. Rather there will be a need for a specific solution for dealing with quality in qualitative research.

### One size fits all?

So how about criteria and strategies for qualitative research in general? Here we find two alternatives in the literature. There is a general discussion about quality criteria or checklists for evaluating qualitative research in general (e.g. Elliot et al., 1999) and there are interventions like that of Reicher (2000) arguing against such generalist approaches and for approach-specific criteria, standards and guidelines. Barbour (2001, p. 1115) speaks of the 'lure of "one size fits all" solutions' in this context. The core of this problem is that the term 'qualitative research' is a kind of umbrella term. Under this umbrella, approaches assemble or are packed that have very different theoretical backgrounds, methodological principles, research issues and aims. What they have in common is sometimes no more than that they are 'not quantitative' in one way or the other.

A general discussion about what good qualitative research is and is not sometimes misses the differences in the approach and aims of different sorts of qualitative research. If we do a grounded theory study using interviews and interested in the contents of everyday knowledge in a specific field, the aim will be to develop a substantial theory from it. In a conversation analysis (see Rapley, 2007) of counselling interaction, the approach is much more focused on the formal principles of this interaction format and the goal is to develop a formal model of such interaction compared to other forms of talk. In both examples, the theoretical backgrounds are as different as the empirical focus and as the overall aim of the studies. Is it possible then to evaluate these two examples with the same criteria once it comes to funding or publication, or do we need different criteria for each, taking the special features of both into account – without becoming completely relativistic in our judgements about good and bad research?

Another distinction to be taken into account is between qualitative research with mainly academic interests (say a dissertation project) and more specific fields like qualitative evaluation (see Flick, 2006b). For example, major inputs to the quality discussion came from Patton (2002) and there are quite a few examples of guidelines for good qualitative evaluation available (see Chapter 2). As well as asking whether methods and approaches from qualitative research in general can be applied to evaluation, we can also ask whether such quality indicators can be transferred one-to-one from evaluation to areas of qualitative research more (or exclusively) interested in discovery or description without evaluation. So the interesting question will be, how to develop approaches to quality in qualitative research that give an orientation across the different fields and approaches and are sensitive to the particulars of the different research traditions.

## *Criteria appropriate to qualitative research or research appropriate to criteria?*

Barbour (2001, p. 1115) mentions another issue relevant in this context. She reports that ' … several researchers have informed me that they must comply with various procedures (such as respondent validation, multiple coding, etc.) in order to satisfy the requirements of specific journals where they hope to publish their work'. Although she doubts how far such claims are accurate or exaggerated, a specific problem of the trend to criteria and guidelines is mentioned here. They could develop a life of their own and they could be used strategically instead of functionally. If certain methods are no longer applied because they are most appropriate to the issue under study but because they make it more likely than other methods to achieve publication in a specific journal, something has gone wrong. If specific strategies or quality criteria are not applied because they are appropriate to what is research or how it is done, but because they make the way into specific journals or towards funding easier, the tail (criteria, checklists) starts to wag the dog (the research), as Barbour puts it. She discusses several examples of research strategies or techniques that have become popular for fitting checklists, journal and funding expectations (respondent validation, multiple coding, triangulation, purposive sampling and grounded theory). Here, we could add the use of programs like ATLAS.ti (see also Gibbs, 2007), which are often mentioned in articles about qualitative research as some kind of method for analyzing the data instead of being seen as a technical device to support an analytic method (like theoretical coding: Strauss and Corbin, 1998). Here I sometimes suspect the idea is that technology use makes qualitative research trustworthy and that the use (and mention) of such technology is more strategic than appropriate.

### How to assess the quality of research in a sensitive and appropriate way

Here, we encounter dilemmas between the needs of the sensitiveness for the particular strengths and features of qualitative research and the needs and interests of actors outside the community in the pure sense – which means commissioners, readers, consumers and publishers of qualitative research. In this book we will focus on several ways of defining, approaching and promoting the quality of qualitative research. These will be located between the formulation and application of criteria, reflections about standards and the formulation and application of strategies. It is important in this context that each of the alternatives – criteria, standards or strategies – is used not only with an eye on scientific claims and interests but that they do justice to what is under assessment – qualitative research – and even more to the people, participants and institutions that are ready to take part in a research. At this crossroads, we find ourselves confronted with the links between quality and ethical issues in qualitative research.

## Ethics and quality of qualitative research

The relation between ethics and quality in qualitative research can be discussed from three angles. From the first, quality is seen as a precondition for ethically sound research. Here we may state that it is unethical to do qualitative research that has not reflected about how to ensure the quality of the research and without being sure that this piece of research will be a good example in the end. Good research is more ethically legitimate as it is worth people investing their time for taking part in it and revealing their own situation or giving an insight into their privacy. If the research is not of high quality in the end, it is unethical to make people take part or reveal their privacy. Ensuring and promoting quality of research becomes a precondition of ethical research in this version.

The second angle sees the reflection of ethical issues (data protection, avoiding harm to participants, respecting perspectives and privacies, and the like) as a quality feature of (qualitative) research. So this sort of ethical reflection becomes a necessary step in the research process (similar to, for example, developing a good set of questions or handling deviant cases, and so on) and should be taken into account when assessing the quality of qualitative research.

And there is a third angle: doing research according to quality standards may affect ethical issues. Making someone recount the whole story of his or her life may be important from a methodological point of view for understanding how a specific illness became part of such a life and how people deal with that illness. The longer and the more detailed such a narrative is developed by the participant in the study – and the more space and support he or she is given in doing so by the research – the better will be the quality of the data that are produced in this way (see Gibbs, 2007). But if the illness is leading to a high vulnerability and exhaustion on the side of the patients, it can be too strong a challenge for them to reflect, recount and reconsider their lives as a whole and in (too much) detail. In such a case, there is a conflict between methodological standards (or quality expectations) and ethical concerns about the confrontation of the participants with certain aspects of their lives. The same can also be the case for approaches such as member checks (see Chapters 2 and 3) or communicative validation (see also Kvale, 2007), which confront participants in a study with what they said (or what the researcher found in analyzing such statements). Both approaches are strategies for increasing quality in qualitative research but can also be an ethical problem in research with vulnerable people.

## Structure of the book

It should have become clear that the issue of quality in qualitative research is raised at different levels with different intentions and consequences. In the remainder of this book, we will address the different approaches to answer the questions linked to the quality issue in qualitative research.

We will deal with the main strategies for managing, that is, ensuring and improving the quality of qualitative research. In the first chapters of the book, we will discuss standards, criteria and strategies for addressing and assessing the quality of qualitative research. In the following chapter, the problem of how to assess the quality of qualitative research and these three alternatives will be unfolded in more detail (Chapter 2). Approaches in the literature to apply validity, reliability and objectivity to qualitative research will be reviewed as well as attempts to set up standards, guidelines and checklists. The approach of strategies for managing quality is addressed for the first time in the next chapter, when we turn to strategies for managing diversity in qualitative research (Chapter 3).

In the second part of the book, the focus will be on triangulation as a strategy for promoting quality in qualitative research. This will lead us through several steps. After discussing the different concepts of triangulation that have been developed over the years (Chapter 4), the use of methodological triangulation in qualitative research in order to enhance its quality is discussed using several examples (Chapter 5). This is outlined in more detail for the field of ethnography (see Angrosino, 2007), again using examples from several areas (Chapter 6).

Qualitative researchers are often confronted with the idea that one way of promoting and assuring quality in their research is to combine it with quantitative research. This has become a topic more recently again in the context of mixed methods research. In Chapter 7, the power and the limits of such combinations in the context of quality promotion will be discussed. The final step in this part addresses practical issues of how to plan and run a study using triangulation with the aim of quality promotion (Chapter 8).

In the final part, strategies of managing transparency, quality and ethics in qualitative research will be the issues. First, we will focus on the relations of quality, creativity and ethics as different ways to ask similar questions (Chapter 9) and approach ethical issues in qualitative research from different angles. In the final chapter (Chapter 10), we will address quality in qualitative research from the angles of the research process and with a focus on the transparency of this process for consumers of a research project (readers, commissioners, students, etc.). Here, the clarification of the indication of qualitative research or of specific variants of it will be discussed in the context of quality management.

## Key points

- The issue of quality in qualitative research is located at the crossroads of internal needs and external challenges.
- It has become a crucial issue with the progressive establishment of qualitative research and in the competition with other forms of research and with other disciplines for funding and publication and influence.
- The formulation of criteria is only one solution to the problem.

## Further reading

In these texts, quality issues for qualitative research are outlined and summarized in some detail with more or less focus on one area (like evaluation) but with relevance for qualitative research as a whole:

Flick, U. (2006a) *An Introduction to Qualitative Research* (3rd edn.). London: Sage, part 7.

Gibbs, G. (2007) *Analyzing Qualitative Data* (Book 6 of *The SAGE Qualitative Research Kit*). London: Sage.

Kvale, S. (2007) *Doing Interviews* (Book 2 of *The SAGE Qualitative Research Kit*). London: Sage.

Patton, M.Q. (2002) *Qualitative Evaluation and Research Methods* (3rd edn). London: Sage, chap. 9.

Rapley, T. (2007) *Doing Conversation, Discourse and Document Analysis* (Book 7 of *The SAGE Qualitative Research Kit*). London: Sage.

Seale, C. (1999) *The Quality of Qualitative Research*. London: Sage.

# 2
# Standards, criteria, checklists and guidelines

**Chapter objectives**
After reading this chapter, you should

- see the problems and limitations in the attempt to set up standards for qualitative research;
- know more about the criteria that are discussed for qualitative research; and
- have an overview of guidelines and checklists suggested for evaluating qualitative research.

## Introduction

The question of how to ascertain the quality of qualitative research has been asked since the beginning of qualitative research and attracts continuous and repeated attention. However, answers to this question have not been found – at least not in a way that is generally agreed upon. Contributions to this discussion include suggestions for formulating quality criteria (see Seale, 1999; Steinke, 2004), or asking for them as the recent ESRC research programs document, or in the more or less laconic statement that answers to such questions have not yet been found (see Lüders, 2004a, 2006a). That, despite the various attempts to solve the problem, such an estimation is still correct, has its reason in the nature of things – the specific situation in which qualitative research currently is.

## What is qualitative research and what are we referring to?

Before entering the discussion of our issue, some remarks are necessary about what the point of reference should be for it. Qualitative research has developed in different contexts. Here we can on the one hand distinguish theoretical and methodological schools. Each of them is characterized by certain basic assumptions, research interests, and – normally but not always resulting from that – methods and methodological preferences. Thus, the approach of grounded theory (see also Gibbs, 2007) was originally developed in the US and can be seen as a qualitative approach in its own right in the Anglo-Saxon but also in the German discussion. The interest in this approach is normally concentrated on developing a theory from empirical material and from analyzing it. Biographical research is in a similar situation; it has developed its own general aim of research – that the analysis of life history should lead to theoretical condensations – and this approach is relevant beyond language boundaries (see Wengraf, 2001; Rosenthal, 2004).

At the same time, we find approaches or schools that are specific for certain contexts and play a major role in these contexts, while they are recognized in other contexts in a very limited way and sometimes do not even look for recognition in these other contexts. Examples are objective hermeneutics or hermeneutic sociology of knowledge, which unfold their impact (and publication efforts) almost exclusively to German-language audiences (but see Reichertz, 2004). Quite similar is the situation for discourse analysis (see Rapley, 2007), which is quite dominant in the UK and has differentiated in various forms there, whereas it has hardly any influence in German discussions (where discourse analysis is associated with other roots). This means that discussions about qualitative research are characterized by several differentiations – schools on the one hand, language-specific thematic priorities and differences on the other hand (see also Flick, 2005, and Knoblauch et al., 2005, for overviews).

This is complemented by (at least) two more differentiations. First of all, we can observe discipline-specific developments. Discourses (on qualitative research) in sociology develop more or less interlocked (or more or less independent) of those in education or in psychology. An example is the *Handbook of Qualitative Research in Psychology* (Willig and Stainton-Rogers, 2007). Of similar relevance is the differentiation among the various fields of application in qualitative research. Here we find areas like qualitative health research (NIH, 2001, Green and Thorogood, 2004), qualitative management and organization research (Cassell and Symon, 2004) or qualitative evaluation (Flick, 2006b; Shaw, 1999). In these fields, the methodological discussions about qualitative research and even more about 'good' qualitative research slowly start to develop separately. This has much to do with the framework conditions under which qualitative research is applied here. Often we have commissioned research that comes with specific expectations as to results and mainly their practical relevance and that has to be realized under different conditions compared to qualitative basic research or research in the context of qualifications (master's or doctoral theses). First of all, we should mention the time limits, which are the background to discussions about the legitimacy of 'shortcut strategies' (see Flick, 2004; Lüders, 2004a) in using qualitative methods in such contexts. A second issue is the question of how to convince target groups – outside the scientific field – with results (see for this Lüders, 2006b).

This brief sketch of the diversification of qualitative research – which was not meant to be exhaustive but rather exemplary and selective – brings us to a dilemma for the discussion about the quality of qualitative research. Questions of how to appropriately define, ascertain or advance this quality are relevant across all these areas. The ways in which it is answered in the different areas, are as different as the needs for clarification and the solutions that are found or suggested. This brings us to the question of whether it can be expected (and seen as appropriate) to find a valid answer to the quality question across the various areas and contexts. It is hardly contested that qualitative research has to find an answer to this question. However, there is a limited consensus of what this answer should look like. Is it to define criteria, which ideally come with benchmarks or cutting edges for differentiating good from less good research? Then the first question is which criteria are appropriate to that, and the next question is whether they should apply to qualitative research as a whole or to specific approaches in qualitative research.

When there are criteria, should they apply in the same way to a grounded theory study as to a discourse analytic study – or also to a case for evaluating an institution? Or has the question of quality in qualitative research to be asked in a fundamentally different way – beyond criteria? Then is the next question, what should replace criteria? In what follows, different approaches to answer the question of quality in qualitative research – with or without criteria – will be presented.

## Standards of non-standardized research

Bohnsack (2005) recently made an interesting suggestion. Here, answering our leading question is linked to how far standards of non-standardized research can be identified or have developed. This discussion is embedded in a more general one about standards in education. Bohnsack shows on the one hand that the standards for non-standardized research cannot be developed in armchair decisions (of methodologists), but have to be derived or made explicit from reconstructing or analyzing the non-standardized or qualitative research practice, which for him is the case for methods of qualitative research, too. ('Thesis 1: Methods and standards of qualitative research are developed on the grounds of empirically reconstructing the research practices' – Bohnsack, 2005, p. 65). That the existing methods of qualitative research have developed from concrete research questions and projects can be easily demonstrated. In the meantime, quite a number of more or less canonized methods in qualitative research have developed and are established. This means that researchers nowadays often face the question, which of these to apply for answering their research questions, and new developments of methods from the research practice are rather the exception. The pertinent question here is: How can we distinguish between good application of existing methods and poor application or unsuitable method selection? For Bohnsack, standards in non-standardized research are second-order standards, which should be developed from analyzing the natural (first-order) standards. If we follow this approach and Bohnsack's argumentation based on it, we can develop standards of qualitative research from analyzing mundane standards of communication and thus reconstruct the criteria 'validity and reliability in qualitative research' (2005, p. 76). His argumentation is that the relevant level of reference for formulating standards is the methodological and theoretical substantiation of each procedure. Bohnsack further argues that we should distinguish qualitative methods into open and reconstructive methods. Only the latter (for an example see Bohnsack, 2004) will meet the quality standards Bohnsack suggests (see thesis 7: 2005, p. 74).

Bohnsack provides quite a number of theoretically and methodologically instructive suggestions for a meta-theoretical foundation of the discussion about the quality of qualitative research. However, several questions remain unanswered. First of all, the question whether the formulation of standards in such a heterogeneous field as qualitative research (in general or already at this moment) can be realized – if there is not even a unity concerning the terminology (qualitative, interpretive, reconstructive) and how far each belongs to the field or not. Second, formulations of standards normally run the risk of coming along with standardizations (of procedures) – which produces at least a contradiction for approaches of non-standardized research. Third – and this will be the decisive argument in our context – questions of assuring or advancing quality are transferred in Bohnsack's way of formulating standards from the level of ascertaining quality in practical procedures in the field to the level of the appropriateness of research programs as a whole. If we apply Bohnsack's suggestion, we may know that certain approaches – reconstructive methods – meet the standards of qualitative research, while others – open methods – do not. Less helpful are these suggestions for finding answers to the question of how to judge concrete applications and procedures in a research project or those reported in an article. This direction is taken by the approaches we will address next.

## Traditional or new criteria to answer the question of qualitative research?

For a long time, it was suggested to take the classical criteria of empirical social research – reliability, validity and objectivity – and to apply them also to qualitative research or to modify them for this area. Kirk and Miller (1986) discuss reliability and validity in this respect. However, on the one hand it becomes clear in this discussion that reliability of data and procedures in the traditional sense – as the stability of data. and results in repeated collections – is rather useless for assessing qualitative data. Identical repetition of a narrative in repeated narrative interviews is rather a sign of a 'constructed' version than of the reliability of what has been told.

Validity (see Kvale, 2007) is also discussed for qualitative research repeatedly. Kirk and Miller (1986, p. 21) summarize the question of validity as whether the researchers see what they think they see. Here too problems arise for an immediate application of classical concepts of validity. Internal validity is increased or ascertained by excluding that other variables than the ones in the hypothesis determine what has been observed. In this concept we already find the reasons for the problems of transferring it to qualitative research. Internal validity is to be advanced by an – if possible – comprehensive control over context conditions in the study. For this purpose, the situations of data collection and analysis are standardized as far as possible. The necessary degree of standardization is not compatible to qualitative methods or questions their actual strengths. In similar ways, it can be shown for other forms of validity why they cannot be transferred directly to qualitative research.

The third criterion from the canon of quantitative research is objectivity. Here we find hardly any attempts to apply this criterion to qualitative research. An exception can be found in Madill et al. (2000). However, objectivity here is exclusively discussed for the analysis of qualitative data and reduced to the question of whether two researchers come to the same results with the qualitative data at hand. Objectivity is interpreted as consistency of meaning, when two or more independent researchers analyze the same data or material. If they arrive at the same conclusions, these can be seen as objective and reliable (p. 17).

Kvale (2007) discusses the objectivity of interviews in four respects: as freedom from bias, as intersubjective consensus, as adequacy to the object and as the object's ability to object.

In summary, even if we find from time to time the claim that qualitative research has to face the questions linked to concepts like reliability and validity (e.g. Morse, 1999, p. 717) or objectivity (Madill et al., 2000), we see in the implementation more attempts to modify or reformulate such concepts.

# Reformulation of traditional criteria

### Reliability of qualitative data

Suggestions for reformulating the concept of reliability go in the direction of a more procedural conception. They aim at making the production of the data more transparent, so that we (as researchers or readers) can check what is still a statement of the interviewee and what is already an interpretation by the researcher. This includes exact and coherent guidelines, how interviews and conversations have to be transcribed (see Gibbs, 2007; Kowal and O'Connell, 2004; Kvale, 2007) or the distinction between verbatim statements in field notes and summaries or paraphrases by the researcher (see Angrosino, 2007). Finally, the reliability of the whole research process can be developed by its reflexive documentation.

### Validation of the interview situation

More differentiated suggestions for judging the validity of interview data, and especially of biographical self-presentations, are made by Legewie (1987, p. 141). According to this author, claims for validity made by a speaker in an interview have to be differentiated (and that means have to be judged separately in terms of the following considerations):

> That the contents of what is said is correct, ... that what is said is socially appropriate in its relational aspect ... and ... that what is said is sincere in terms of the self-presentation of the speaker. The point of departure for validating biographical statements is to analyse the interview situation for how far 'the conditions of non-strategic communication' were given and whether 'goals and particularities of the interview ... are negotiated in the form of a more or less explicit ... 'working contract'. (1987, pp. 145–9)

The main question here is whether the interviewees were given any cause to consciously or unconsciously construct a specific, that is, biased version of their experiences that does not or does only correspond with their views in a limited way. The interview situation is analyzed for any signs of such deformations. This should provide a basis for finding out which systematic deformations or deceptions in the text are a result of the interview situation and how far and how exactly they have to be taken into account in the interpretation. You can further extend such reflections on the side of the researcher by involving the interviewee.

### Communicative validation

Another version of specifying validity aims at involving the actors (subjects or groups) in the further research process. One way is to introduce communicative validation at a second meeting after the interview and its transcription (see Chapter 3). The promise of further authenticity made here is twofold. The interviewees' agreement with the contents of their statements is obtained after the interview. The interviewees themselves develop a structure of their own statements in terms of the complex relations the researcher is looking for (see also Kvale, 2007).

For a more general application of such strategies, however, two questions remain to be satisfactorily answered. First, how can you design the methodological procedure of communicative validation in such a way that it really does justice to the issues under study and to the interviewees' views? Second, how can the question of grounding data and results further be answered beyond the subjects' agreement? One way of proceeding here is to attempt to develop a more general reconstruction of the concept of validation.

### *Procedural validation*

Mishler (1990) goes one step further in reformulating the concept of validity. He starts from the process of validating (instead of from the state of validity) and defines 'validation as the social construction of knowledge' (1990, p. 417), by which we 'evaluate the "trustworthiness" of reported observations, interpretations, and generalizations' (1990, p. 419). Finally, 'reformulating validation as the social discourse through which trustworthiness is established elides such familiar shibboleths as reliability, falsifiability, and objectivity' (1990, p. 420). As an empirical basis for this discourse and the construction of credibility, Mishler discusses the use of examples from narrative studies.

Altheide and Johnson (1998) suggest a concept of 'validity as reflexive accounting', which creates a relation between researcher, issues and the process of making sense and locates validity in the process of research and the different relationships at work in it:

1  the relationship between what is observed (behaviours, rituals, meanings) and the larger cultural, historical, and organizational contexts within which the observations are made (the substance);
2  the relationship among the observer, the observed, and the setting (the observer);
3  the issue of perspective (or point of view), whether the observer's or the members', used to render an interpretation of the ethnographic data (the interpretation);
4  the role of the reader in the final product (the audience);
5  the issue of representational, rhetorical, or authorial style used by the author(s) to render the description and/or interpretation (the style). (1998, pp. 291–2)

Thus, validation is regarded from the perspective of the whole research process and the factors that are involved. However, the suggestions remain on the programmatic level rather than that concrete criteria or guiding principles are formulated for assessing single studies or parts of them. All in all, attempts at using or reformulating validity and validation face several problems. Formal

**17**

analyses of the way the data were produced, for example in the interview situation, do not tell us anything about the contents of these interviews and whether they have been appropriately treated in the further proceeding of the research. The concepts of communicative validation or member checks face a special problem. The subjects' consent becomes problematic as a criterion where the research systematically goes beyond the subject's viewpoint, for example in interpretations that wish to permeate into social or psychological unconsciousness or that derive from the distinctiveness of various subjective viewpoints.

Kvale (2007) summarizes the different versions of reformulating validity in several statements: To validate is to investigate, is to check, is to question and is to theorize. Validity is reformulated into communicative validity and pragmatic validity. Valid then no longer means to define an abstract criterion and to match results and procedures with it, but is turned into a reflection at several levels, while valid is what finds the consensus of members and what works in the field.

The attempts to reformulate the concept of validity, which were discussed here, are marked by a certain fuzziness that does not necessarily offer a solution for the problem of grounding qualitative research but rather provides questioning and programmatic statements. As a general tendency, a shift from validity to validation and from assessing the individual step or part of the research towards increasing the transparency of the research process as a whole may be stated. Whether it makes sense or not to apply classical criteria to qualitative research is questioned, because 'the "notion of reality" in both streams of research is too heterogeneous' (Lüders and Reichertz, 1986, p. 97). A similar reservation can already be found in Glaser and Strauss; they

> raise doubts as to the applicability of the canons of quantitative research as criteria for judging the credibility of substantive theory based on qualitative research. They suggest rather that criteria of judgement be based on generic elements of qualitative methods for collecting, analyzing and presenting data and for the way in which people read qualitative analyses. (1965, p. 5)

From this scepticism, a series of attempts has been made over time to develop 'method-appropriate criteria' in order to replace criteria like validity and reliability.

## Alternative, method-appropriate criteria

A third way of answering the question of how to assess the quality of qualitative research is to look for alternative, method-appropriate criteria. Here, the idea is that the question of quality in general can and should be answered by using criteria, but that the traditional criteria miss the features of qualitative research and methods.

Lincoln and Guba (1985) suggest trustworthiness, credibility, dependability, transferability and confirmability as criteria for qualitative research. The first of these criteria is considered to be the main one. They outline five strategies for increasing the credibility of qualitative research:

- activities for increasing the likelihood that credible results will be produced by a 'prolonged engagement' and 'persistent observation' in the field and the triangulation of different methods, researchers and data;
- 'peer debriefing': regular meetings with other people who are not involved in the research in order to disclose one's own blind spots and to discuss working hypotheses and results with them;
- the analysis of negative cases in the sense of analytic induction (see Chapter 3);
- appropriateness of the terms of reference of interpretations and their assessment;
- 'member checks' in the sense of communicative validation of data and interpretations with members of the fields under study (see Chapter 3).

Thus, a series of starting points for producing and assessing the procedural rationality in the qualitative research process is outlined. In this way, proceedings and developments in the process of research can be revealed and assessed. In terms of the findings that have already been produced in a particular piece of research, the questions answered through the use of such an assessment procedure can more generally be summarized as follows, according to Huberman and Miles (1998):

- Are findings grounded in the data? (Is sampling appropriate? Are data weighed correctly?)
- Are inferences logical? (Are analytic strategies applied correctly? Are alternative explanations accounted for?)
- Is the category structure appropriate?
- Can inquiry decisions and methodological shifts be justified? (Were sampling decisions linked to working hypotheses?)
- What is the degree of researcher bias (premature closure, unexplored data in the field notes, lack of search for negative cases, feelings of empathy)?
- What strategies were used for increasing credibility (second readers, feedback to informants, peer review, adequate time in the field)? (1998, p. 202)

Although the findings are the starting point for evaluating the research, an attempt is made to do this by combining a result-oriented view with a process-oriented procedure.

The strategies outlined so far aim at formulating criteria that can be used in qualitative research in analogy to those established in quantitative research. Steinke (2004) has suggested criteria for qualitative research in a more comprehensive approach:

- intersubjective transparency of the process that led to the results;
- indication and appropriateness of the procedures;
- empirical anchoring of theory building and testing;
- limitation, i.e. defining the range and limits of results;
- reflected subjectivity; coherence of the theory and relevance of the research question and the theory development (see also Chapters 3, 9 and 10 below).

A more specific suggestion comes from Charmaz (2006, pp. 182–3) for evaluating grounded theory studies. She suggests four criteria, each of which comes with several questions.

### Credibility
- Has your research achieved intimate familiarity with the setting or topic?
- Are data sufficient to merit your claims? Consider the range, number and depth of observations contained in the data.
- Have you made systematic comparisons between observations and between categories?
- Do the categories cover a wide range of empirical observations?
- Are there strong logical links between the gathered data and your argument and analysis?
- Has your research provided enough evidence for your claims to allow the reader to form an independent assessment – and *agree* with your claims?

### Originality
- Are your categories fresh? Do they offer new insights?
- Does your analysis provide a new conceptual rendering of the data?
- What is the social and theoretical significance of this work?
- How does your grounded theory challenge, extend or refine current ideas, concepts and practices?

### Resonance
- Do the categories portray the fullness of the studied experience?
- Have you revealed both liminal and unstable taken-for-granted meanings?

- Have you drawn links between larger collectivities or institutions and individual lives, when the data so indicate?
- Does your grounded theory make sense to your participants or people who share their circumstances? Does your analysis offer them deeper insights about their lives and world?

## *Usefulness*

- Does your analysis offer interpretations that people can use in their everyday worlds?
- Do your analytic categories suggest any generic processes?
- If so, have you examined these generic processes for tacit implications?
- Can the analysis spark further research in other substantive areas?
- How does your work contribute to knowledge? How does it contribute to making a better world? (Charmaz, 2006, pp. 182–3)

Charmaz does not unfold this set of criteria in greater detail, but defines some links between them: 'A strong combination of originality and credibility increases resonance, usefulness and the subsequent value of the contribution' (p. 183). Her list is a combination of process criteria addressing the quality of the study (credibility), relevance criteria (resonance and usefulness) and novelty criteria (originality).

The suggestions briefly presented here face several problems: First – and in contrast to the assessment of reliability in quantitative research, for example – it is difficult here to define benchmarks or indicators for distinguishing between good and bad research. In the case of credibility suggested by Lincoln and Guba, only strategies for how to produce or increase the credibility are suggested. Researchers who want to apply these strategies for advancing the quality and credibility of their research are left alone with the following question, as are the readers who want to assess a reported research with this criterion: Which results should the peer debriefing and/or member checks produce for being an indicator for the credibility of the research assessed with it? Is it necessary that all peers or members involved come to the same evaluations – for example of the plausibility of results – or is it sufficient if a majority or certain persons confirm such a plausibility? Should the confirmation by certain persons be given more weight than the rejection by other members or peers? This becomes relevant as the idea of criteria without the formulation of benchmarks degenerates into well-meant formulations of intentions (see also Lüders, 2004a). At the same time, all these suggestions have been formulated against the background of a specific approach in qualitative research and are limited in their application to other approaches.

# Guidelines, checklists and catalogues of criteria

As we saw in Chapter 1, the question of how to assess the quality of qualitative research is currently raised in three contexts: It comes up for researchers who want to assess and ascertain their results; it becomes relevant for users of research – readers of publications, commissioners of funded research – who want to (and often have to) assess and evaluate what is presented to them as results after the funding has ended; and in the evaluation and reviewing of qualitative research, in reviewing research proposals and increasingly in reviewing manuscripts in the peer review process of journals. Particularly in the last context, a growing number of guidelines for assessing research papers (articles, proposals) are developed, used and published in different fields of application.

## Health research

Seale (1999, pp. 189–92) presents a criteria catalogue of the British Sociological Association/Medical Sociology, which includes a set of questions referring to 20 areas from research questions to sampling, collection and analysis of data or presentations and ethics. The guiding questions are helpful, but if you want to answer them, you are drawn back to your own – maybe implicit – criteria for example, when you want to answer in area 19 ('Are the results credible and appropriate?') the question 'do they address the research question(s)?' (p. 192).

Another catalogue has been presented by the National Institutes of Health Office of Behavioral and Social Sciences (NIH, 2001) for the field of public health. Here, especially, questions of design have been emphasized. Analysis and interpretation are summarized under design as well as the combination of qualitative and quantitative research. A checklist complements the catalogue. This includes items like 'Data collection procedures are fully explained' (p. 16).

Elliot et al. (1999) have developed a catalogue of guidelines for publishing qualitative research, in two parts. One can be applied both to quantitative and qualitative research, the second part is focused on the special character of qualitative research and includes concepts like member checks, peer debriefing triangulation, and so on. But as the strong reaction of Reicher (2000) shows, these guidelines, despite their rather general formulation, are not consensual for different forms of qualitative research.

## Qualitative evaluation

Particularly for the context of qualitative evaluation, in the last few years more and more checklists, frameworks and criteria catalogues have been developed (see also Flick, 2006b; Patton, 2002). For example, Spencer et al. (2003) have presented a 'framework for assessing research evidence' for this area. It is based on analyses of the literature and 29 expert interviews with commissioners, recipients, researchers and practitioners involved in evaluations. The framework is oriented on four guiding principles. Research should be

- contributory in advancing wider knowledge or understanding;
- defensible in design by providing a research strategy which can address the evaluation questions posed;
- rigorous in conduct through the systematic and transparent collection, analysis and interpretation of qualitative data;
- credible in claim through offering well-founded and plausible arguments about the significance of the data generated. (2003, p. 6)

For assessing concrete projects, the authors have formulated a total of 18 questions, which can be allocated to seven areas or steps of the research process. Such questions refer to the results (e.g. How credible are the findings? How has knowledge/ understanding been extended by the research?), to designs and sampling (e.g. How well defended is the sample design/target selection of cases/documents?) and to data collection and analysis (e.g. How well has the approach to and for-mulation of the analysis been conveyed? Contexts of data sources – how well are they retained and portrayed?). The presentation of results and the researcher's reflexivity and neutrality are also issues of questions. While these questions have a more orienting function, the framework is made concrete in the 'quality indica-tors' provided with them. Here we find a total of 88 with different numbers for the single questions. For the question referring to credibility, for example, we find the indicator 'Findings/conclusions make sense/have a coherent logic', for sample com-position the indicator 'Detailed profile of achieved sample/case coverage', each of them complemented by other indicators (for the complete list see Spencer et al., 2003, pp. 22–4).

This catalogue of questions was commissioned by the 'Research Cabinet' and 'the UK Government's Office of the Chief Social Researcher' (Kushner, 2005, p. 111) and sent out to ministries and all government departments. It was to give them an orientation for commissioning and even more for assessing evaluations based on qualitative methods. In particular, because of this distribution and func-tion, Kushner (2005) for example regards the framework with particular attention and critically. She sees different advantages, for example that the framework brings some clarification to the area of evaluation or that it is a contribution to further developing qualitative research in methodological terms and to save eval-uators from unreasonable contracts and commissions (pp. 15–16). More impor-tant, however, are the reservations she formulates. Kushner in general criticizes that the formulation and distribution of such assessment instruments lead to a shift in the responsibility for quality from the evaluators to the commissioners (often administrations): '… it places on government an unreasonable responsi-bility to manage and guarantee the independence of an evaluation. Independence is conventionally guaranteed by the principle that an evaluation externally is "sponsored" and not "bought" by government' (p. 116).

Furthermore, Kushner criticizes that the considerations in the framework are based too much on the epistemological and methodological literature but hardly aim at the 'politics of inquiry' or of the evaluators' mandate. In particular, the confrontation with multiple and/or conflicting intentions is not taken enough into account: 'There is, for example, no discussion of the propensity for qualitative evaluation to uncover multiple and often conflicting purposes, often bringing to question the partiality of programme objectives' (p. 116).

In summary, Kushner sees that the framework is too much oriented on questions of applied social research and not enough on the particularities of qualitative evaluation (that these are two different things is outlined, for example, by Lüders, 2006b). Also it focuses more on the epistemological than on the practical dimension of evaluation and equates 'policy evaluation' with program evaluation. Kushner derives the question of ownership from this: who owns an evaluation – the commissioner or the evaluator?

In this considerable and detailed suggestion of a catalogue for assessing qualitative evaluations and the detailed critique of it, we can see the problematic of assessing the quality of qualitative studies again. Here too, questions are raised of whether such catalogues should (and can) be applied to all forms of evaluations (policy versus program evaluation), of how to break down the more fundamental discourse about quality to a manageable instruction in the research practice, which at the same time takes the particularities of evaluation compared to (other) research into account. Finally – and something that has not been further considered by Kushner in her critique – the (appraisal) questions and quality indicators suggested in the framework are more orienting questions than suggestions for defining the border between good and bad evaluation. Criteria in quantitative research include such benchmarks normally; a certain degree of correlation between coders has to be reached in the assessment of inter-rater reliability if the criterion is to be met. And finally we could ask, what relevance the framework and the accompanying considerations have for qualitative research beyond evaluation.

### Management and organization research

For this area, Cassell et al. (2005) have run a project on 'Benchmarking good practice in qualitative management research'. They interviewed consumers of such research and elaborated their implicit and explicit standards of assessing qualitative research. They found the interviewees' concepts of what qualitative research is about and how the credibility of its results is assessed. For the latter, we find aspects like how far results can be quantified, the rigorous use of methods, the availability of 'technical skills' in running the project, and that practically relevant conclusions could be drawn from the results, and so on. 'Good practice' in qualitative research is mainly seen in aspects like the research design (why was the method chosen, how was the sampling conceptualized?) and whether combinations of methods (mainly qualitative and quantitative) have been applied. Furthermore, the analysis and reflexivity of the selected procedures and the presentation and distribution of results become relevant for assessing the whole research. In defining the quality of qualitative management research, the question of which 'contribution' has been made with the results is central: do they provide new insights, practical consequences or the discovery of new problems as results? But also aspects like 'technical accomplishment' in the application of methods or the question of how far criteria in running a project played a role are seen as relevant.

This study mainly shows which implicit and explicit criteria the consumers of results from qualitative research in a specific area apply. It can be read as a contribution to the social science utilization research – which again shows that practitioners apply different standards and criteria in evaluating results and procedures in research than researchers do (see also Lüders, 2006a). At the same time it shows that researchers themselves should define what good qualitative research is, because otherwise the evaluation of qualitative research develops (even more) a momentum of its own or is defined from the outside. Finally, this project shows the problems that arise if we want to reconstruct the standards of research from the standards in the field or in the practical area, as Bohnsack (2005) suggests (see above). This research team, for example, has not managed to develop convincing criteria, standards or a catalogue for assessing research projects and results from their analysis.

The assessment catalogues that were briefly outlined here are less a final answer to the question for appropriate criteria for evaluating qualitative research. Rather they demonstrate the explosive power of the quality question for qualitative research and that it is asked more and more concretely and that answers may be imposed on qualitative research from the outside, if it does not provide such answers itself.

## Strategies as an alternative to formulating criteria

A third alternative – beyond formulating standards or criteria – is to develop and apply strategies of quality promotion for increasing the quality of data and findings. This extends the focus of the quality question from assessing a single step in the research process to addressing the process as a whole. This will be the focus in what follows.

### ▤ Key points

- Diversification and proliferation of qualitative research makes it more difficult to develop universal criteria and standards for qualitative research in general.
- Standards will only be helpful, if they apply to qualitative research in general and not only to specific approaches.
- Traditional criteria tend to miss the specific qualities of qualitative research. Alternative criteria mostly come without benchmarks for distinguishing good research from bad examples.
- Guidelines and checklists are rejected by many qualitative researchers for various reasons.
- Strategies of quality promotion are an alternative way of addressing quality in qualitative research.

## Further reading

The following works give overviews of attempts to formulate, use, reformulate or reject criteria in qualitative research:

Flick, U. (2006a) *An Introduction to Qualitative Research* (3rd edn). London: Sage, part 7.

Gibbs, G. (2007) *Analyzing Qualitative Data* (Book 6 of *The SAGE Qualitative Research Kit*). London: Sage.

Kvale, S. (2007) *Doing Interviews* (Book 2 of *The SAGE Qualitative Research Kit*). London: Sage.

Patton, M.Q. (2002) *Qualitative Evaluation and Research Methods* (3rd edn). London: Sage, chap. 9.

Rapley, T. (2007) *Doing Conversation, Discourse and Document Analysis* (Book 7 of *The SAGE Qualitative Research Kit*). London: Sage.

Seale, C. (1999) *The Quality of Qualitative Research*. London: Sage.

# 3
# Strategies for managing diversity

**Chapter objectives**
After reading this chapter, you should

- see the relevance of using the strategies presented here for the promotion of quality in qualitative research; and
- see the quality issue as something to develop by using such strategies rather than something to measure and state by criteria.

## Introduction

As should have become evident so far, it is not so easy to answer the quality question in qualitative research in the way we are used to from quantitative research. Neither has it been easy to formulate and define criteria for qualitative research that are widely accepted and close to becoming standards for the different approaches of qualitative research. Nor has it been possible to define standards of qualitative research that are convincing and that can be applied to different forms of (qualitative) research. The *via regia* in quantitative research for addressing and managing quality issues is a standardization of the research situation and to rely on abstract rather than concrete parameters – like using a random sample instead of purposive sampling, to make the application of methods independent from the person applying them, and suchlike. These strategies cannot simply be applied to qualitative research without giving up its strengths; standardization is counterproductive for research situations that are living from a relatively flexible use of methods. In general, qualitative researchers are more interested in specific cases (people, situations, etc.) and not in a random selection of material. The researcher as a person becomes an important part of any research situation in qualitative research. Whereas the leitmotifs of quality promotion in quantitative research are standardization and in some respects abstraction, in qualitative research the leitmotifs are rather diversity, flexibility and concreteness in order to extend the knowledge potential of research settings rather than reducing biases and influences. In the remainder of this book, different strategies for managing and producing diversity in the data and analyses will be in the focus. In this chapter, we will address strategies for managing diversity (from the angle of the quality question), before the second part of the book focuses on a strategy for deliberately producing a wider range of diversity.

## Theoretical sampling

Theoretical sampling is a basic strategy in qualitative research for collecting material. Glaser and Strauss describe this strategy as follows:

> Theoretical sampling is the process of data collection for generating theory whereby the analyst jointly collects, codes and analyses his data and decides what data to collect next and where to find them, in order to develop his theory as it emerges. This process of data collection is controlled by the emerging theory. (1967, p. 45)

In our context, it becomes relevant in so far as it is oriented to open a space for diversity in the research process. This aims at covering a fuller range of possible variations in the field and in the phenomenon under study. Charmaz (2006) has given an updated definition:

> Theoretical sampling means seeking pertinent data to *develop* your emerging *theory*. The main purpose of theoretical sampling is to elaborate and refine the categories constituting your theory. You conduct theoretical sampling by sampling to develop the properties of your category(ies) until no new properties emerge. (2006, p. 96)

This sampling strategy – if applied rigorously – prevents researchers from reducing their phenomenon under study prematurely to a specific pattern based on (too) similar cases (or materials). Although Charmaz insists that theoretical sampling is not sampling to find negative cases (p. 100, see below), a strength of theoretical sampling is that it allows for negative cases coming into the sample according to the developing theory. Therefore she suggests:

> Conduct theoretical sampling after you have already defined and tentatively conceptualized relevant ideas that indicate areas to probe with

more data. Otherwise, early theoretical sampling may result in one or more of the common grounded theory pitfalls:

- Premature closure of analytic categories
- Trite or redundant categories
- Over-reliance on overt statements for elaborating and checking categories
- Unfocused or unspecified categories. (2006, p. 107)

If theoretical sampling is applied consistently, it has as a consequence: 'Variation within a process becomes apparent while you are conducting theoretical sampling' (2006, p. 109). Theoretical sampling allows introducing diversity and variety in the data. As Glaser and Strauss as well as Charmaz underline, it should always be driven by theory – the state of the developing theory in the study. Therefore it is basically an approach that aims at building a bridge between the structure developing (in the theory) and the variance existing (in the field or phenomenon). As such it becomes a crucial step in the research process on which it depends, however open the process remains for what is happening in the field and however long the process remains open for such a diversity.

## Analytic induction

Once enough diversity has been established in the selection and the collection of the data, it becomes relevant, from the angle of quality in qualitative research, how this diversity is managed, maintained and taken into account in analyzing the data. The aim of all research is to identify some kind of generality – patterns, typologies, structures, systems, models, and the like. This sort of 'generalization' comes with a reduction of varieties; a multitude of cases will be ordered and comprised according to a limited number of types or patterns. Sometimes this generalization starts by formulating tentative hypotheses, which are then tested against the material and further developed. Testing such hypotheses does not mean the same as in the context of experimental research. In qualitative research, a hypothesis is more like a working hypothesis. Testing here means more to assess such a working hypothesis, or a model, pattern, and so on, for its fitting to the empirical material and for how far it covers the range in the material. If the typology or the patterns are exhaustive and well developed, they will cover each and every case – ideally.

Research practice, however, shows that in most projects you will for example find a typology with several cases matching the types one to one, while other cases do not fit perfectly to one type or even to the whole typology. So there are fitting and deviant cases. Then the question is, how to deal with this issue – cases that do not fit to a general pattern that has been developed or a pattern that does not apply to (or cover) all the material that was collected. This is where analytic induction (introduced to social science and research by Znaniecki, 1934) becomes relevant. Analytic induction explicitly starts from a specific case. According to Bühler-Niederberger (1985), it can be characterized as follows: 'Analytic induction is a method of systematic interpretation of events, which includes the process of generating hypotheses as well as testing them. Its decisive instrument is to analyse the exception, the case, which is deviant to the hypothesis' (1985, p. 476).

This procedure of looking for and analyzing deviant cases is applied after a preliminary theory (hypothesis, pattern, model, etc.) has been developed. Analytic induction above all is oriented to examining theories and knowledge by analyzing or integrating negative cases. The procedure of analytic induction includes the steps in Box 3.1.

---

**Box 3.1    Steps of analytic induction**

1   A rough definition of the phenomenon to be explained is formulated.
2   A hypothetical explanation of the phenomenon is formulated.
3   One case is studied in the light of the hypothesis with the object of determining whether the hypothesis fits the facts in that case.
4   If the hypothesis does not fit the facts, either the hypothesis is reformulated or the phenomenon to be explained is re-defined so that the case is excluded.
5   Practical certainty may be attained after a small number of cases has been studied, but the discovery by the investigator or any other investigator of a single negative case disproves the explanation and requires a reformulation.

This procedure of examining cases, re-defining the phenomenon and reformulating the hypothesis is continued until a universal relation is established, each negative case calling for a re-definition or a reformulation.

Source: Cressey (1950).

---

In this concept, several aspects are interesting for a methodology oriented to promoting quality of qualitative research. First of all, it includes the explicit use of hypotheses. These hypotheses are formulated for better understanding of what is happening in the data, for structuring the data and for explaining the phenomenon under study. They are tentative and revised against the material. This is already mentioned by Angell and Turner, when they see analytic induction as a method 'in which the investigator does not accept ready-made conceptualization, but plays around with the relationships and the units of analysis until he hits upon a scheme that is very parsimonious in explanatory power' (1954, p. 476).

The second relevant aspect is the focus on specific cases, in particular deviant cases. Accordingly, Lincoln and Guba (1985) refer to this concept as the 'analysis of negative cases'. Using analytic induction as a strategy forces the researcher to make differences between certain cases and a general tendency or a structuring principle explicit and also to remedy the lack of fitting between case(s) and structure. Used in such a way, it prevents researchers from using categories and categorical system too loosely and to overlook or ignore diversities in the material.

Thirdly, analytic induction is a way to take the exception as a point of reference rather than the average and normality in the material.

Goetz and LeCompte (1981) give a description of its use and outline a rather radical understanding of analytic induction:

> This strategy involves scanning the data for categories of phenomena and for relationships among such categories, developing working typologies and hypotheses upon an examination of initial cases, then modifying and refining them on the basis of subsequent cases. ... Negative instances, or phenomena that do not fit the initial function, are consciously sought to expand, adapt, or restrict the original construct. In its most extreme application, analytic induction is intended to provide universal rather than probabilistic explanation; that is, all cases are to be explained, not merely some distribution of cases. (1981, p. 57)

This description of how to proceed is a very good description of the application of analytic induction, even if their account of an extreme application refers more to exceptions than to regular uses of this concept.

Going in a similar direction, Denzin (1989) sees several advantages of analytic induction:

> *First*, it allows researchers to disprove theories while testing one theory against another. ...
> *Second*, analytic induction provides a method by which old theories can be revised or incorporated into new theories as negative evidence is taken into account. ...
> *Third*, this method, with its extreme emphasis on importance of the negative case, forces a close articulation between fact, observation, concept, proposition and theory.
> *Fourth*, analytic induction provides one direct means, by which theoretical and statistical sampling modes of sampling can be brought together; that is, investigators will find themselves extending their propositions to representative cases not yet examined. ...
> *Fifth*, analytic induction allows the sociologist to move from substantive, or middle-range, theories to formal theories. ...

**31**

> *Sixth*, analytic induction leads to developmental or processual theories, and these are superior to static formulation, which assume that variables operate in either an intervening or an antecedent fashion on the processes under study. (1989, pp. 169–70)

Much of the critique raised upon this concept refers to claims to identify (and prove) causes for phenomena by giving unambiguous explanations (see Robinson, 1951, for example). Rather, its fruitfulness for current qualitative research is not so much in a falsification of theories or explanation by contradictory facts or negative cases, but the impulse to further elaborate models, patterns and the like so as to make them cover a wider range of phenomena. This can already be found in Znaniecki's early formulations:

> If a datum is merely viewed as a 'contradictory instance', i.e., as an individual case in which a hypothesis presumed true proves false, it is scientifically unproductive, so all it does is to impair the logical validity of the hypothesis and force us to substitute a particular for a general judgment. But if we base upon it another general hypothesis, we go beyond mere contradiction, we have two positive conflicting theories to choose from and the choice can be decided only by introducing new evidence – previously unknown or neglected elements, characters, connections or processes. Thus, further research is made indispensable, and out of it emerge new hypotheses and new problems. (1934, pp. 281–2)

There are links to questions of generalization of case studies, but analytic induction has its own importance as a procedure for assessing analyses. All in all, analytic induction or the use of negative cases is a specific elaboration of what is discussed by Glaser (1969) as the constant comparative method. It focuses on a two-sided comparison: cases with cases and cases against theoretical models, patterns, and so on. With the concentration on cases not supporting what has been developed theoretically so far, it forces the researchers to critically examine and scrutinize their own reflections and thoughts about what they study. The idea of analytic induction can be extended beyond the somehow schematic use of 'negative *cases*' to analyzing and specifically reflecting instances, observations, statements and the like that do not completely or easily fit into a developing structure. In such a sense, negative case techniques and analytic induction become techniques for managing diversity in the research process and for seeking further clarification of such diversity.

The consequences of applying this strategy to material that has been collected and analyzed can be multiple: first, the readjustment of the analysis to the deviant cases; second, the search for new material (for example, other cases similar to the deviant cases); and third, the move to a different method, for example to do interviews when observations produced a structure but also deviant cases (Bloor, 1978).

## Members' and audiences' consensus

As in the example of Bloor (1978), we can use two ways out of discrepancies arising from analyzing negative cases or applying analytic induction. One is to seek members' consensus or validation. The second is to use different methods (see the later chapters of this book). Member checks are 'the most crucial technique for establishing credibility' for Lincoln and Guba (1985, p. 314). This technique has been discussed by using different labels, sometimes with different intentions. Labels are communicative validation (see Chapter 2), respondent validation, member check, member validation, consensual validation, and so on. The common feature is that consensus of participants is taken as a criterion or as an indicator for assessing research products – from data to results. Bloor (1997) notes three basic forms of member validation:

> The validation of the researcher's taxonomies by the attempted predic-
> tion of members' descriptions in the field ... ; the validation of the
> researcher's analysis by the demonstrated ability of the researcher to
> 'pass' as a member ... ; the validation of the researcher's analysis
> by asking collectivity members to judge the adequacy of the
> researcher's analysis, taking results back to the field and asking 'if the
> members recognize, understand and accept one's description'
> (Douglas, 1976, p. 131), (Bloor, 1997 p. 41).

Seale (1999, p. 62) sees two versions of asking 'members to judge the adequacy of the researcher's account: (a) strong version (e.g. members evaluate the final research report); (b) weak version (e.g. members comment on the accuracy of some interim document, such as an interview transcript)'.

In the semi-standardized interview developed by Groeben and Scheele (see Groeben, 1990; Flick, 2006a, chap. 13), researchers seek members' consensus referring to the main statements in the interview. For this purpose, their (individual) main statements are presented back to the individual participants in the study and they are asked to accept, reject or modify these statements. Here, it is neither the results nor the transcripts of the interview that are fed back to the participant, but a condensation of what he or she has said in the interview.

In this example, members' consensus is obtained for the single case and referring to the data, not to interpretations (although a condensation is already a form of interpretation). Lincoln and Guba (1985, pp. 373–6) suggest member checks at the end of the study and not referring to the single case but to the overall results. They call their approach a 'comprehensive member check' and set up a review panel consisting of participants in the study (who acted as interviewees previously, for example) and non-participants. For the former, it is important to have representatives of all stakeholding groups and of all sites, local settings and institutions in the panel. All in all, as many different perspectives as possible should be included in the panel and members should join it for as long a period as possible. Then the information presented to the panel has to be prepared, which should focus on a case or on selected excerpts of the analysis and come with consent forms and comment sheets. The review of the material and the meeting of the panel should provide three forms of feedback: a judgment of overall credibility, statements about major concerns about the results, and statements about factual or interpretive errors in the analysis (p. 377). Agreement can be distinguished in three versions: complete consensus, split consensus (by some part or subgroup in the panel) and majority consensus with a (strong) minority dissent. Finally, it is important to consider the inputs coming from such a member-check process in the final analysis and report, that is, to develop ways of taking members' suggestions seriously. (In Chapter 5, an example will be presented of how to use focus groups for such a member check with the participants of a study based on interviews in the first part.)

Such attempts at using participants' consensus as an indicator for the credibility or validity of research (products) have several features and several problems in common. First, it is common to them that they follow Kvale's (2007) dictum 'To validate is to communicate'. Second, research is made more dialogical by introducing such a step. Third, it can become more relevant, as this form of checking back with members always includes feeding back results to participants, to the field, to practical contexts and the like. Fourth, they liberate the participants from a passive role as objects of research and take them seriously as an active partner in the process – by making them members in the process.

At the same time, these approaches face similar problems in the dialogue with the members. First, it has turned out to be necessary to find a way of 'translating' research discourse and documents into mundane or practical discourse. For example, most people are at least irritated when they read a transcript of an interview they gave, because of the difference between spoken and written language, which makes it difficult to read verbatim protocols of what you have said. This produces irritation on the part of the participants, which has to be overcome before they can validate anything in such a situation. If you take results back to members you should find a way to make them comprehensible to your specific group of participants. Then the question arises, what to bring back to the individual participant: results referring to this specific person or more general results like a typology, for example. In the latter case, what is it that the participant consents or validates: his or her location in such a typology (I belong to type I – yes or no), the plausibility of such a typology according to his or her experience or its practical relevance? In the case of validating results with members, we often face the problem that our interpretations go beyond what they see or perceive and that such an interpretation can include a confrontation with aspects in their knowledge or practices that they were not aware of before.

Second, the status of such a consensus should be reflected. Will it be the only criterion or way of validating what the researcher has found? Then in the case of rejection by the member, are the research and its result obsolete? Is it still possible to produce findings that go beyond what members see or have already seen before? And what is the knowledge progress of research compared to mundane knowledge? This leads to the third problem: how to integrate rejections of results by participants, how to manage this form of diversity in the continuation of the research process. What if some participants agree, others reject, and the rest do not know what to think of what they are presented with? So member validation in this strict sense of the word will give diversity a space to come up and forces the researcher to develop ways of handling such a diversity in the ongoing research.

An alternative and/or addition can be the use of peer debriefing for improving the quality of research and for collecting a different view on one's own proceeding. In funded research and in publications, peer reviews play a more and more important role, but these reviews are mostly anonymous and are judgements rather than commentaries and dialogues. Peer debriefing means to seek discussions with other researchers or experts about one's own research and the advances in it. Lincoln and Guba (1985) suggest peer debriefing for the development of research designs, for discussing working hypotheses and for discussing results. Here again, peer debriefing is a way to collect second opinions, different views and diversity in the perspectives on the material and the research process.

## Conclusion

The strategies discussed in this chapter are ways of managing diversity in the research process – from the inclusion and selection of empirical material in the step of sampling, to the use and treatment of negative cases in analytic induction, to the search for comments and consensus from other parties in member checks and peer debriefing. Common to these strategies is that they establish and manage a certain relation from the theoretical advancements of a study to conflicting materials: cases to include according to or developing these advancements, cases that resist these advancements initially, and opinions in the field that may contradict these theoretical advancements. Management of diversity includes strategies that overcome fast and premature insights and explanations drawn from materials, their analysis and the fields under study. These strategies go beyond the use of criteria, although the strategies are sometimes discussed as parts of criteria (in Lincoln and Guba, 1985) or addressed by checklists (see Chapter 2). To see and to use them as strategies (rather than as criteria) avoids the (false) promises of providing easy to handle cut-off points and benchmarks for distinguishing good from bad research. This also allows using them more as ways of managing and promoting quality rather than simply judging it. In their conceptualization, these strategies remain open for being used in and adapted to different approaches in qualitative research. They can be complemented by strategies of triangulation as ways of systematically extending the perspective in the research process, which will be discussed in the following chapters in some detail.

## ▤ Key points

- Quality in qualitative research is only possible if the researchers allow room for diversity in what they study – if they take deviant cases into account in their analysis and avoid a premature exclusion or neglect of such diversity.
- Theoretical sampling is not only a way to interesting material but also a way for opening the door for diversity in the field to come into the researcher's data.
- To search members', audiences' and peers' consensus is also a way to allow their dissent with what researchers did, found and concluded and thus a way to different and differing views.

### Further reading

In the following texts, analytic induction and member checks are unfolded in more detail than is possible here:

Flick, U. (2006a) *An Introduction to Qualitative Research* (3rd edn). London: Sage.
Kvale, S. (2007) *Doing Interviews* (Book 2 of *The SAGE Qualitative Research Kit*). London: Sage, part 7.
Lincoln, Y.S. and Guba, E.G. (1985) *Naturalistic Inquiry*. London: Sage.
Seale, C. (1999) *The Quality of Qualitative Research*. London: Sage.

# 4
# Concepts of triangulation

**Chapter objectives**
After reading this chapter, you should know

* the background and the different versions of triangulation and see its relevance for managing quality in qualitative research;
* the different lines of discussion referring to this concept and its use in quality and other contexts in qualitative research; and
* that triangulation has been a feature of many good examples of qualitative research – at least implicitly.

## Triangulation in the history of qualitative research

Triangulation is a concept that is often taken up in qualitative research when issues of quality are discussed. The major link between triangulation and quality of qualitative research is that triangulation means extending the activities of the researcher in the process beyond what is 'normally' done, for example, by using more than one method. The different ways of extending the research activities with the aim of quality promotion will be unfolded in this and the following chapters in some detail. For this, we will address the theoretical and conceptual basis of triangulation in this chapter before the use of different forms of triangulation is discussed in the following ones. Different aims, and sometimes myths and reservations are linked to triangulation. Sometimes it is discussed when qualitative research is combined with quantitative approaches in order to give its results more grounding. In general, discussions of triangulation began in the 1970s when Norman Denzin (1970) presented a more systematic conceptualization of triangulation. If we go back a little further in the history of qualitative research, we will find that many of the studies seen as classic studies in qualitative research have not used the concept explicitly but were run according to the principles and practices of what is now discussed as triangulation. We may also find that such practices of triangulation can be seen as a feature of qualitative (also including the use of quantitative) research, as some examples may show.

The study of Marie Jahoda, Paul Lazarsfeld and Hans Zeisel (1933/1971), *Marienthal: The Sociology of an Unemployed Community*, is one of the classic studies in qualitative research (see also Fleck, 2004). Here, psychological coping with unemployment in a village was studied in the late 1920s after the main employer of its inhabitants went bankrupt. The result is the elaboration of the leitmotif of a 'tired society' as a condensed characterization of the attitude towards life and the day-to-day practices in the village and of different types of practices in reaction to the unemployment (for example, the 'unbroken', the 'resigned', the 'desperate' and the 'apathetic'). The methodological procedures leading to these insights have been summarized by Jahoda (1995, p. 121) in the four rules:

1   For catching social reality, qualitative and quantitative methods are indicated.
2   Objective facts and subjective attitudes should be collected.
3   Observations at present should be complemented by historical material.
4   Unconspicuous observation of spontaneous life and direct, planned interviews should be applied.

These principles include linking different methodological approaches (qualitative, quantitative, interviews and observation). At the same time, we find different methodological perspectives (objective facts, subjective attitudes, current and historical issues). In describing the study (1971), the authors list the data they used: cadastre sheets of about 500 families, life histories, sheets for documenting the use of time, protocols, school essays, different statistical data, and historical information about the village and its institutions. Accordingly, Lazarsfeld (1960, p. 14) has made the link between qualitative and quantitative data and strategies a principle at least for this study. According to Lazarsfeld (1960, p. 15), 'three pairs of data' were used for the analysis: 'natural sources' (statistics of library use) and data, which were collected for research purposes (sheets of time use); 'objective indicators' (e.g. health statistics) and subjective statements (interviews); and 'statistics and empathic descriptions of single cases'.

Another early example of triangulation of verbal and visual data is the study of Gregory Bateson and Margaret Mead (1942). A remarkable feature is the empirical approach of producing and analyzing more than 25,000 photographs, masses of filmed material, paintings and sculptures on the one hand and using ethnographic conversations about this material on the other hand. Also, in *The Polish Peasant in Europe and America* by Thomas and Znaniecki (1918–1920), different sorts of data were combined: 'undesigned records' as well as an exemplary life history produced by a participant for the study. Morse (2003, p. 190) finally sees the work of Goffman (e.g. 1989) as an example for applying triangulation without using the term. These examples show that the use of different sorts of data was characteristic of many classic studies at the beginning of qualitative research.

Barney Glaser and Anselm Strauss and their approach of discovering grounded theories were at the core of the renaissance of qualitative research in the 1960s in the US and in the 1970s in Europe. Not only the methodological works, but also the studies (e.g. Strauss et al., 1964), are influential and instructive. Again we find different hints for the use of what was later named triangulation. Glaser and Strauss suggest the use of different types of data:

> Different kinds of data give the analyst different views or vantage points from which to understand a category and to develop its properties; these different views we have called *slices of data*. While the sociologist may use one technique of data collection primarily, theoretical sampling for saturation of a category allows a multi-faceted investigation, in which there are no limits to the techniques of data collection. (1967, p. 65)

They also suggest using many different sorts of data, whereas Strauss et al. (1964, p. 36) advocate employing different observers in order to increase the reliability of observations that were made independently of each other and comparing them.

These examples may show that the triangulation of data sources, of methods and of researchers has a long tradition in various areas of qualitative research, even if the term was not (yet or always) used. These examples also demonstrate that, in the tradition of these studies, triangulation as an empirical approach to fields and issues was employed as an instrument assessing empirical results as well as a way to more insights and knowledge and to managing and promoting quality in the research.

Triangulation becomes particularly important in both ways when training in empirical methods increasingly includes qualitative and quantitative research and keywords like 'mixed methods' (Tashakkori and Teddlie, 2003a) develop a special appeal. Here again, we should examine critically whether they can really meet expectations of a pragmatic and at the same time theoretically founded combination of research approaches – in producing knowledge and in assessing the quality of research and results. In this context, the question becomes relevant how far the concept of triangulation has a special importance in the combination of reflection and pragmatism. In this and the following chapters, triangulation as a methodological strategy will be inspected and further spelled out against the background of the research traditions and in the context of the current discussions. The special focus here is on its use and relevance in the discussions about quality of qualitative research. Therefore it should not only become clear what triangulation is and how it can be applied, but also what it is not and which problems can arise by using it for enhancing and ensuring the quality of qualitative research.

## What is triangulation and what is not?

Put simply, the concept of triangulation means that an issue of research is considered – or in a constructivist formulation is constituted – from (at least) two points. Normally, the consideration from two or more points is materialized by using different methodological approaches (see Chapter 5). The concept of triangulation was imported from land surveying and geodesy, where it is used as an economic method of localizing and fixing positions on the surface of the earth (see Blaikie, 1991, p. 118). The definition used in this context is:

> Triangulation is the method of location of a point from two others of known distance apart, given the angles of the triangle formed by the three points. By repeated application of the principle, if a series of points form the apices of a chain or network of connected triangles of which the angles are measured, the lengths of all the unknown sides and the relative positions of the points may be computed when the length of one of the sides is known. (Clark, 1951, p. 145)

In a more metaphorical sense, Campbell and Fiske (1959) and Webb et al. (1966) introduced triangulation into general methodological discussion in the social sciences. At that point, the idea was already that the issue under study is also constituted by the methods used to study it. At that time, the rather negative reading was dominant: that the issue is possibly biased by the methods that are used and that results have to be seen as artefacts. The leading question was, 'if a hypothesis can survive the confrontation with a series of complementary methods of testing' (Campbell and Fiske, 1959, p. 82). This led to considerations of how to prevent such a bias, and 'unobtrusive' and 'nonreactive measurement' (Webb et al., 1966) were stipulated. One strategy was the combination of different measurements and methods – in a 'multitrait-multimethod-matrix' (Campbell and Fiske, 1959). In this context, the metaphor of triangulation is imported 'from navigation and military strategy that use multiple reference points to locate an object's exact position' (Smith, 1975, p. 273).

For a better understanding of the concept of triangulation, it might be helpful to see what is *not* meant by it. In combining methods, it does not mean that one method is used for collecting data (e.g. an interview) and another one (e.g. coding) is used for analyzing those data. This is obvious and does not need an extra term. Neither does it mean the exploratory use of qualitative methods before the actual study using a standardized method, if the exploratory study is not seen as a genuine and stand-alone part of the project, but is only used for developing a questionnaire and the results of the first step do not become part of the final results of the whole study.

## Definition of triangulation

What is to be understood as triangulation in the context of social science and especially of qualitative research (see Box 4.1)? This understanding of triangulation will be further unfolded by using the different concepts that are used in the discussion of social science methodology and elaborated in later chapters in its concrete implementation.

---

**Box 4.1**   Definition of triangulation

Triangulation includes researchers taking different perspectives on an issue under study or more generally in answering research questions. These perspectives can be substantiated by using several methods and/or in several theoretical approaches. Both are or should be linked. Furthermore, it refers to combining different sorts of data against the background of the theoretical perspectives that are applied to the data. As far as possible, these perspectives should be treated and applied on an equal footing and in an equally consequent way. At the same time, triangulation (of different methods or data sorts) should allow a principal surplus of knowledge. For example, triangulation should produce knowledge at different levels, which means they go beyond the knowledge made possible by one approach and thus contribute to promoting quality in research.

---

# Multiple Triangulation

## Aims of triangulation

In discussions in qualitative research, triangulation has attracted most attention with the conceptualization by Denzin (1970, 1989). Originally, Denzin sees triangulation generally as '… the combination of methodologies in the study of the same phenomena' (1970, p. 297). The aims of triangulation are for Denzin:

> Triangulation, or the use of multiple methods, is a plan of action that will raise sociologists above the personalistic biases that stem from single

methodologies. By combining methods and investigators in the same study, observers can partially overcome the deficiencies that flow from one investigator and/or method. Sociology as a science is based on the observations generated from its theories, but until sociologists treat the act of generating observations as an act of symbolic interaction, the links between observations and theories will remain incomplete. In this respect triangulation of method, investigator, theory, and data remains the soundest strategy of theory construction. (1970, p. 300)

## Data triangulation

Denzin distinguishes various forms of triangulation. 'Data triangulation' refers to the use of different sources of data as distinct from using different methods in the production of data (1970, p. 301). Triangulation of data allows the researcher to reach a maximum of theoretical profit from using the same methods. Denzin differentiates data triangulation in different ways: he suggests studying the same phenomenon at different times, in various locations and with different persons. Denzin thinks that this strategy is comparable with theoretical sampling by Glaser and Strauss (1967). In both cases, a purposive and systematic selection and integration of persons, populations, and temporal and local settings is employed.

Beyond that, Denzin distinguishes three levels at which we can analyze persons in empirical research: (1) In surveys, individuals are often randomly sampled and linked statistically to other cases without reference to a specific context. (2) Interactions in groups, families or teams are the second level. Here, the interaction and not the (single) person is the point of reference. (3) Persons are studied as parts of collectivities, for example, members of organizations, social groups or communities. Here persons and interactions are only regarded as units in so far as they represent pressures or demands coming from the collectivity (1970, p. 302).

## Investigator triangulation

As a second form, Denzin suggests 'investigator triangulation'. This means that different observers or interviewers are employed to reveal and minimize biases coming from the individual researcher. The following example from Strauss et al. may illustrate this strategy.

There were three fieldworkers subjected for the most part to the same raw data. Search for pinpointing and negative evidence was abetted by the collective nature of our inquiry. If the colleague reported the same kind of observation as another without prior consultation, confidence grew. If after hearing the report of an observation, a colleague was himself able unquestionably to duplicate it, it indicated that our observational techniques had some degree of reliability. If no colleague did corroborate an observation – which did happen – if it seemed important then, or later, further inquiry was initiated. Something like a built-in relia- bility check was thus obtained because several fieldworkers were exposed directly to similar or identical data. (1964, p. 36)

However, this does not mean simply sharing the work or delegating routine prac- tices to auxiliary workers, but the systematic comparison of different researchers' influences on the issue under study and on the results of studying it:

When multiple observers are used, the most skilled observers should be placed closest to the data. Triangulating observers removes the poten- tial bias that comes from a single person, and insures a greater reliability in observations. ... (Denzin, 1970, p. 303)

### Theory triangulation

The third type in Denzin's classification refers to

... approaching the data with multiple perspectives and hypotheses in mind. Data that would refute central hypotheses could be collected, and various theoretical points of view could be placed side by side to assess their utility and power. (1970, p. 303)

Again, the scope of knowledge is to be extended and put on a more solid ground. Especially in fields characterized by a low degree of theoretical coherence, the use of theoretical triangulation is suggested. Denzin refers to situations in which different theories are available to explain a phenomenon. Then you can try to confirm one or the other theory with the data (facts speaking for themselves: Westie, 1957) or choose the theory that seems to be most plausible or develop your own theory from the data (Denzin, 1970, p. 302). Theory triangulation becomes relevant when it is applied to a concrete set of data, for example an inter- view protocol. Examples of such a theory-comparative approach to data from different perspectives is, for example, to analyze an interview with different methods of text interpretation, which takes the theoretical background assump- tions of each method into account, of each method or the researcher using them. That very varied interpretations result from such an approach is not so surprising if we take the concept of Denzin seriously. He comes to the conclusion from a (hypothetical) example: '... each perspective directs analysis to different data areas, suggests different research methods and contradicts the explanations of the other' (1970, p. 306).

The advantages of theory triangulation are, according to Denzin, that it prevents researchers from sticking to their preliminary assumptions and from ignoring alternative explanation. For this, it is necessary to make all the assumptions and theories to hand at the beginning of a study (1970, p. 306). In addition to that, sociologists using theory triangulation go beyond theory-specific studies toward generalized theoretical studies (1970, p. 306). And finally, theory triangulation promotes progress in theory and research by a comparative assessment and maybe falsification of rival theoretical models through a purposive analysis of 'negative evidence' or through developing theoretical syntheses (p. 307).

### Triangulation of methods

The strongest attention is paid to the fourth form suggested by Denzin – methodological triangulation. Again, Denzin distinguishes two alternatives: within-method and between-methods triangulation. As an example of the first, he mentions different subscales in a questionnaire for addressing the same issue. For the second, he pursues the discussion about the combination of different methods in order to limit their reactivity (according to Webb et al., 1966), when he requires overcoming the limitations of the single methods by combining them. Denzin formulates a series of principles of methodological triangulation:

> The nature of the research problem and its relevance to a particular method should be assessed. ... As methods are adapted to the special problems at hand, their relative strengths and weaknesses must again be assessed. ... It must also be remembered that each method has unique strengths and weaknesses. ... Methods must be selected with an eye to their theoretical relevance. ... To maximize the theoretical value of their studies, investigators must select their strongest methods. ... Researchers must be flexible in the evaluation of their methods. Every action in the field provides new definitions, suggests new strategies, and leads to continuous modification of initial research designs. ... No investigation should be viewed in a static fashion. (1970, pp. 308–10)

In these principles, Denzin suggests not so much a naïve-pragmatic combination of methods but rather a very methods-critical process of selecting methods and a continuous assessment of methodological decisions and of their appropriateness (see Flick, 2006a, for this). The point of reference is the ('special') issue of research and the theoretical relevance of the research questions and of the results of a study. Nevertheless, at that time, the focus of methodological triangulation was for Denzin above all to validate field research, as the following summary shows:

> To summarize, methodological triangulation involves a complex process of playing each method off against the other so as to maximize the validity of field efforts. Assessment cannot be solely derived from principles given in research manuals – it is an emergent process, contingent on the investigator, his research setting, and his theoretical perspective. (1970, p. 310)

Finally, Denzin outlines some problems of planning studies with multiple triangulation:

> The first and most obvious problem is locating a common unit of observation against which various theories can be applied. ... The only solution is to select one common database and simply force the theories to be applied to those data. ... A second problem may be that restrictions of time and money make it impossible to employ multiple observers, multiple methods, and multiple data sources. ... A final problem involves the inaccessibility of critical data areas, types, or levels. (1970, pp. 311–12)

Problems mentioned here refer mainly to the accessibility of fields of research in which triangulation can be applied with the necessary consistency, and to the danger that triangulation might over-challenge the – however limited – resources of a study (see Flick, 2007, and Chapter 8 below).

Denzin has made a comprehensive proposal for designing and applying triangulation. His original concept in the 1970s moved back and forth between the claim for validating results (by playing off methods against each other), the increase in the reliability of procedures (several methods are more reliable than one method) and the grounding of theory development through the different forms of triangulation. At some points, the constitution of issues by methods is neglected. Denzin repeatedly talks of applying methods to the 'same phenomenon'. In response to some of the discussions and critiques that will be presented next, and due to changing his methodological position in general, Denzin has modified some aspects of his concept of triangulation in later editions of his book *The Research Act* (1989; see below).

## Lines of discussion

Denzin's approach to triangulation is not only the most often quoted and discussed. Also, most of the critiques of triangulation refer directly to it. A first starting point is the concept of issues underlying the combination of different methods. Starting from an ethnomethodological position, Silverman issues as a caveat:

> ... we have to be careful about inferring a master reality in terms of which all accounts and actions are to be judged. This casts great doubt on the argument that multiple research methods should be employed in a variety of settings in order to gain a 'total' picture of some phenomenon ... Putting the picture together is more problematic than such proponents of triangulation would imply. What goes on in one setting is not a simple corrective to what happens elsewhere – each must be understood in its own terms. (1985, p. 21)

Mainly, he criticizes that – despite his actually interactionist position – Denzin assumes that different methods represent the 'same phenomenon' and that we only have to put together the resulting parts of the picture. If we follow the critique of Silverman, Denzin ignores the point that was at the beginning of the whole discussion of triangulation – for example, in the case of Webb et al. (1966), the reactivity of methods, or in different terms, that every method constitutes the issues to be studied with it in a specific way. The consequence is that a combination of surveys and field research (Fielding and Fielding, 1986), participant observation and interviews (Hammersley and Atkinson, 1983) or more generaly qualitative and quantitative research will not necessarily lead to the 'same' results and that discrepancies in results falsify one or the other finding. On the contrary, such a discrepancy results from the relation of method and issue in the single method, which makes it necessary to develop criteria for assessing congruences and discrepancies in the results. Only then can the following critique by Fielding and Fielding be ignored: 'Multiple triangulation as Denzin expounded it, is the equivalent for research methods of "correlation" in data analysis. They both represent extreme forms of eclecticism' (1986, p. 33).

The phenomenon under study will be marked by the researcher's theoretical conceptualization in the way it can be perceived. This conceptualization influences how methods are designed and used and the interpretation of data (observations, answers, etc.) and results. Denzin takes this into account in his idea of theoretical triangulation. He neglects this in the (only methodological) use of triangulation as a strategy of validation by playing methods off against each other. Triangulation as a 'quasi-correlation' is in danger of ignoring or neglecting the implications of a theoretical position and of a use of methods resulting from this. The reason for this is that triangulation was (mis-)understood as a form of validation at the beginning. Thus, Fielding and Fielding condense their critique of Denzin's conception in the following programmatic argumentation:

> Theoretical triangulation does not necessarily reduce bias, nor does methodological triangulation necessarily increase validity. Theories are generally the product of quite different traditions so when they are combined, one might get a fuller picture, but not a more 'objective' one. Similarly different methods have emerged as a product of different theoretical traditions, and therefore combining them can add range and depth, but not accuracy. (1986, p. 33)

Such an understanding of triangulation suggests seeing it less as a strategy of validation than as an alternative to it. Accordingly, Fielding and Fielding conclude:

> In other words, there is a case for triangulation, but not the one Denzin makes. We should combine theories and methods carefully and purposefully with the intention of adding breadth or depth to our analysis but not for the purpose of pursuing 'objective' truth. (1986, p. 33)

Here, triangulation still has the function of contributing to further grounding of data and interpretation. This aim is pursued via more adequacy and comprehensiveness in grasping the issue under study and not by a unilateral or mutual validation of the single results.

In the next step we will address the question, which form of congruence of results can be achieved with triangulation? If methods that are used have different qualities, it is not so much identical results that we should expect. Rather it is complementary or convergent results that can be expected (see Flick, 2004; Kelle and Erzberger, 2004). Convergence means that results fit into each other, complement each other, lie on one level, but do not have to be congruent (Lamnek, 1988, p. 236). This means giving up the claim that triangulation – as an equivalent to correlation – allows validating methods in results in a traditional sense. If you want to assess the complementarity of results, much more – theoretical – effort is necessary than if you want to assess congruence via correlation numerically.

In the context of qualitative research, we cannot expect such unambiguous results and criteria for judging the reliability of single methods and results. Rather we should expect an extension of knowledge potential and rather an extended than a reduced need for (theory-driven) interpretation, as Köckeis-Stangl makes clear: 'Instead of talking about validations, perhaps it would be more adequate to see our control processes as more perspective triangulation … and to be prepared in advance for receiving as a result no uniform picture but rather one of a kaleidoscopic kind' (1982, p. 363).

All in all, the critique of Denzin's early concept of triangulation has focused on the idea of validating by playing off methods against each other. In particular, his assumption that different methods simply represent an object, which will be the same for every method used to study it, was criticized. Sometimes this is still the argument when triangulation in general is discussed (see Bryman, 1992, or Tashakkori and Teddlie, 2003b). While updating his approach to triangulation and revising his methodological stance in general in a very comprehensive way (see Lincoln, 2004; Denzin, 2004), he has taken up some of the critical points.

## Triangulation as sophisticated rigor: Denzin's reaction to his critics

In his more recent publications (e.g. Denzin, 1989, p. 246; Denzin and Lincoln, 1994, p. 2), Denzin sees triangulation in a more differentiated way. At the core of his updated version is the concept of 'sophisticated rigor':

> Interpretive sociologists who employ the triangulated method are committed to *sophisticated rigor*, which means that they are committed to making their empirical, interpretive schemes as public as possible. This requires that they detail in careful fashion the nature of the sampling

framework used. It also involves using triangulated, historically situated observations that are interactive, biographical, and, where relevant, gender specific. The phrase *sophisticated rigor* is intended to describe the work of any and all sociologists who employ multiple methods, seek out diverse empirical sources, and attempt to develop interactionally grounded interpretations. (1989, pp. 235–6)

Denzin still sees the claim for triangulation overcoming the methodological limitations of single methods (1989, p. 236). At the same time, he gives up the idea of playing off methods against each other in order to test hypotheses and reacts to Silverman's (1985) critique:

Accordingly, data triangulation better refers to seeking multiple sites and levels for the study of the phenomenon in question. It is erroneous to think or imply that the same unit can be measured. At the same time, the concept of hypothesis testing must be abandoned. The interactionist seeks to build interpretations, not test hypotheses. (Denzin, 1989, p. 244)

In reaction to Fielding and Fielding (1986), Denzin reformulates the aims of multiple triangulation:

The goal of multiple triangulation is a fully grounded interpretive research approach. Objective reality will never be captured. In-depth understanding, not validity, is sought in any interpretive study. Multiple triangulation should never be eclectic. It cannot, however, be meaningfully compared to correlation analysis in statistical studies. (Denzin, 1989, p. 246)

All in all, in his later writings, Denzin sees triangulation as a strategy on the road to a deeper understanding of an issue under study and thus as a step to more knowledge and less toward validity and objectivity in interpretation.

## Systematic triangulation of perspectives

The suggestion of a 'systematic triangulation of perspectives' (Flick, 1992) goes in a similar direction. Here, different research perspectives in qualitative research are triangulated in order to complement their strengths and to show their limits. The aim is not a pragmatic combination of different methods, but to take into account their theoretical backgrounds. The starting points for this suggestion are classifications of the varieties of approaches in qualitative research, which are a basis for a theoretically founded, systematic triangulation of qualitative approaches and perspectives. This will be illustrated with a study about subjective theories of trust and their use in counselling practices, which I did some time ago. In this study, I applied an interview in order to reconstruct subjective theories of counsellors. Later I applied communicative validation for the contents of these theories and conversation analysis to consultations done by the same counsellors. The methodological issues of this study will be taken up in more detail in Chapter 5. Here, the theoretical and methodological background of the triangulation of different methods will be the focus.

## Research perspectives in qualitative research

A starting point is that there is no longer *one* single qualitative research, but that different theoretical and methodological perspectives of research with different methodical approaches and theoretical conceptions of the phenomena under study can be identified within the field of qualitative research. Several attempts to structure this field with its variety of methods and their theoretical and methodological backgrounds have been undertaken.

Lüders and Reichertz (1986, pp. 92–4) bundle up the current variety of qualitative research in research perspectives 'aiming at (1) the understanding of the subjective sense of meaning, (2) at the description of social action and social milieus and (3) at the reconstruction of in-depth-structure generating meanings and actions'. For the first perspective, the concentration on the respondent's viewpoint and experiences and the 'maxim to do justice to the respondent in all phases of the research process as far as possible' are characteristic features. These goals are mostly pursued by using interview strategies. In the second perspective, methodical principles are 'documenting and describing different life-worlds, milieus and sometimes finding out their inherent rules and symbols', which are realized for instance through conversation analysis. In the third perspective, subjective sense, intentions and meanings as surface phenomena are differentiated from objective in-depth structures as an own level of reality that generates actions. This differentiation is methodologically realized mostly by using hermeneutic methods (Reichertz, 2004).

Bergmann (1985) distinguishes 'reconstructive methods' (for example, interviews or participant observation) and (in a strict sense of the term) 'interpretive methods' (like conversation analysis) as fundamentally different approaches. While the first group of methods is employed to *produce* data (by questions or interventions in the field) in order to *reconstruct* events and participants' viewpoints for the purpose of research, in the second group research activities are restricted to merely *record and analyze* social activities in their 'natural form'. Each of these approaches discloses or obstructs different points of view on the phenomena under study.

Other authors suggest comparable taxonomies of qualitative research (see also Flick, 2006a, for this). These taxonomies can be used as a starting point for a triangulation of qualitative approaches that can be founded in research perspectives.

## Triangulation of various qualitative strategies

These examples show that there are different streams of qualitative research with distinctive understanding of methods and issues and with different theoretical backgrounds. This can be used for a more appropriate approach to the issue under study. Here, triangulation becomes relevant as 'an attempt to relate different sorts of data' (Hammersley and Atkinson, 1983, p. 199).

## Systematic triangulation of perspectives and the sorts of data to use

Accordingly, Fielding and Fielding (1986, p. 34) suggest combining methods that capture structural aspects of a problem under study with those that focus on the essential features of its meaning for the participants. If we transfer this idea to the differentiations of qualitative research mentioned before, we should combine methods that allow producing sorts of data

- which allow understanding subjective meanings and a description of social practices and milieus,
- while using an interpretive approach to social practices should be combined with a reconstructive approach to analyze viewpoints and meanings beyond a current situation or activity.

As indicated before, these differentiations (from Fielding and Fielding to Bergmann) can be combined at a methodological level by using conversation analysis together with interviews. Then we can reach the first aim in each differentiation with conversation analysis, the second by using interviews. Triangulating these two approaches may be seen as one example of putting the intended diversity of perspectives into concrete methodological terms. Examples of other combinations could be developed (see Table 4.1). This triangulation of research perspectives allows combining methodological approaches like interviews and conversation

TABLE 4.1   Systematic triangulation of perspectives

| Authors | Perspective I | Method I, for example | Perspective II | Method II, for example |
|---|---|---|---|---|
| Bergmann (1985) | Interpretive approaches | Conversation analysis | Reconstructive approaches | Interviews |
| Lüders and Reichertz (1986) | Description of social practices and social milieus | Conversation analysis | Understanding subjective sense of meaning | Interviews |
| Fielding and Fielding (1986) | Structural aspects of the problem | Conversation analysis | Meaning of the problem for those involved | Interviews |

analysis or interviews and participant observation in a systematic way (see Chapters 5 and 6 for examples).

## Comprehensive triangulation

After outlining the approach of a systematic triangulation of perspectives, we can take up the original suggestions by Norman Denzin and his four alternatives of triangulation. This can then be developed into a more systematic model, which includes these alternatives as elements of a chain (see Table 4.2).

TABLE 4.2    Comprehensive triangulation

- Investigator triangulation
- Theory triangulation
- Methodological triangulation

  - within method
  - between methods

- Data triangulation
- Systematic triangulation of perspectives

Researchers interested in using the full potential of triangulation should include different researchers (investigator triangulation), either working in collaboration or independently. Ideally they would bring in different theoretical perspectives, which will lead to one of the versions of methodological (within or between methods) triangulation. The result would be a triangulation of different sorts of data, which then allows a systematic triangulation of perspectives, if theoretical backgrounds and different aspects of the phenomenon under study are included in the approach. How far this whole chain can be pursued in the single research project should depend on the issue under study, the research question, and the resources in the project (see Chapter 8). Even if realized only in part, this strategy can contribute to managing and promoting the quality of qualitative research.

## Triangulation between constructing issues, producing knowledge and assuring results

From the theoretical and methodological discussions about the concept of triangulation that we have outlined here, several conclusions can be drawn for our context. The critiques of Denzin's original concept make clear that we should take into account that every method constitutes its issue in a specific way. Simple congruence in studying the 'same' object should not be expected from triangulating different methods. Rather, a triangulation of different methodological approaches can show different forms of constituting an issue, which may complement or

51

contradict each other. Triangulation does not produce congruent or contradictory representations of an object, but shows different constructions of a phenomenon – for example, at the level of everyday knowledge and at the level of practices. Triangulation will be appropriate and elucidating when not only methods are linked, but also the theoretical perspectives attached to them. As the discussions so far have shown, a contemporary concept of triangulation will include not only an assessment of validity of results, but also the collection of more knowledge.

Finally, it is legitimate to talk of triangulation if the different approaches have the same relevance in planning a study, collecting and analyzing the data, and if they are applied consistently. The different concepts of triangulation outlined in this chapter provide a basis for a reflected use of this strategy in the context of quality promotion in qualitative research. Common to them is that triangulation should be more than a simple and pragmatic combination of two or more methods and that we should avoid a 'more of the same' strategy in triangulation. If we start from a systematic triangulation of perspectives, the contribution to quality promotion will be most fruitful. In the following chapters, we will transfer this discussion to a more methodological level and continue our discussion with respect to the level of research practice, when we address several alternatives of how to make methodological triangulation work.

## Key points

- Triangulation has a history in qualitative research not only but mainly in the context of quality promotion.
- For reaching the latter, is seems necessary to spell out the concept of triangulation in more detail.
- The discussion of the concept has led to more differentiation and to a switch from using triangulation as a strategy of validation to more reflection and more knowledge as a contribution to quality.
- Triangulation will be methodologically sound if we take into account that we implicitly combine research perspectives when combining methods.
- It will be even sounder if we apply this combination of research perspectives more explicitly as a basis for selecting methods to combine in order to promote quality in qualitative research.
- Comprehensive triangulation is an approach to using the methodological potential of this strategy most consistently when it comes to terms of managing quality in qualitative research.

## Further reading

Triangulation and its theoretical basis are spelled out in more detail in the following sources:

Denzin, N.K. (1989) *The Research Act* (3rd edn). Englewood Cliffs, NJ: Prentice-Hall.

Flick, U. (1992) 'Triangulation revisited: strategy of or alternative to validation of qualitative data', *Journal for the Theory of Social Behavior,* 22: 175–97.

Flick, U. (2004) 'Triangulation in qualitative research', in U. Flick, E.von Kardorff and I. Steinke (eds), *A Companion to Qualitative Research.* London: Sage, pp. 178–83.

# 5
# Methodological triangulation
# in qualitative research

**Chapter objectives**
After reading this chapter, you should understand

- the principles of combining different approaches in one method;
- the links between theory triangulation and methodological triangulation; and
- the relevance of both for promoting quality in qualitative research.

When triangulation is discussed in the context of quality issues in qualitative research, most authors refer to methodological triangulation. The basic idea here is that using more than one method will open up several perspectives for promoting quality in qualitative research compared to a single methods study. Here again, we find different suggestions of how to combine different methods and which sorts of methods should be combined. Denzin already distinguished in his concept of triangulation between 'within methods' and 'between methods', and the latter meant the triangulation of several stand-alone methods. In what follows, the first strategy will be spelled out a little more by using several examples, before the triangulation of several (qualitative) methods is discussed. Denzin (1970) mentions the example of using different subscales in a questionnaire as an example for within-methods triangulation.

# Within-methods triangulation: the case of the episodic interview

If we apply this idea to qualitative research, it means combining different methodological approaches in one qualitative method. These approaches include different aims and theoretical backgrounds, but do not go beyond the scope of one method (see Fig. 5.1).

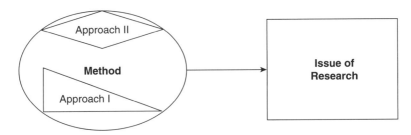

FIGURE 5.1    Within-methods triangulation

Depending on how method or methodological approach is understood, we could use ethnography as an example also (see Angrosino, 2007, and Chapter 6 below). Here, method is to be understood as a procedure combining different methodological approaches. As an example of this form of triangulation I will discuss the episodic interview (see Flick, 2000a, 2006a). This method combines questions and narratives in approaching a specific issue, for example, everyday knowledge about techno-logical change (see Flick, 1994, 1995) or health concepts of lay people (see Flick, 2000b) or of professionals (see Flick et al., 2003, 2004c).

## *Triangulation of theoretical perspectives in one method*

This method was developed against a specific theoretical background, which is informed by more recent discussions and findings of the psychology of memory and knowledge. Here we find a distinction between narrative-episodic and semantic-conceptual knowledge. The first is more oriented to situations, their context and progress, whereas the second knowledge is more abstract, generalized and decontextualized from specific situations and events and oriented to concepts, defini-tions and relations. The first can be accessed more easily in narratives, the second more easily with (argumentative) statements. Narratives (see Kvale, 2007) are more context-sensitive for the context in which experiences are made than other, more semantic models of knowledge. However, knowledge that abstracts more from such contexts is developed from a multitude of similar, generalizable experiences – for example, as knowledge of concepts and rules. More so than in narratives, which are centred upon the particular (Bruner, 1990, 2002), semantic knowledge represents the normal, rule-based and generalized knowledge across a multitude of situations and experiences. This again is episodically concretized and fleshed out in narrative knowledge: 'Rules and maxims state significant generalisations about experience but stories illustrate and explain what those summaries mean' (Robinson and Hawpe, 1986, p. 124).

These abstract parts of knowledge are rather grouped around conceptual meanings and their (semantic) relations. This does not mean that narrative knowledge would not aim at meanings. The term 'semantic knowledge' has been used for some time following models of semantic memory and is based on a rather limited concept of meaning compared to narrative knowledge (Bruner, 1990). Semantic models of knowledge were conceptualized following models of semantic memory, which have been studied in the cognitive psychology of memory for some time. Tulving gives as a definition:

> Semantic memory is the memory necessary for the use of language. It is a mental thesaurus, organized knowledge a person possesses about words and other verbal symbols, their meaning and referents, about relations among them, and about rules, formulas, and algorithms for the manipulation of these symbols, concepts and relations. (1972, p. 386)

If we transfer this principle to the various models of semantic knowledge developed over time, we can summarize that they consist of concepts linked by semantic relations. Similar to memory, semantic-conceptual knowledge is complemented by episodic parts. The starting point is Tulving's (1972) juxtaposition of semantic and episodic memory, which, in addition to concepts, includes memories of concrete situations. It is central for a conception of episodic memory or knowledge that it is not concepts and their relations that are the basis, but memories of specific situations, events or cases from one's own experience. That means that a central feature of knowledge and memory according to this approach are concrete situations with their components: location, time, what happens, who is involved, and so on. For the contents of episodic knowledge it should be stated that it consists not only of autobiographical memory but of situation-related knowledge in general (Strube, 1989). This situational knowledge in the episodic knowledge or memory is the basis for 'generalising across concrete events, which produces general knowledge from episodic knowledge by decontextualisation and this general knowledge has lost the memory of time and localization' (1989, p. 12). General experiential knowledge is based on the generalisation of knowledge, which was first collected and stored in reference to situations. It has lost its situational specificity when it is transferred to other, similar situations and general concepts and rules of interrelations have developed. Both parts are complementary parts of world knowledge. This means that 'world knowledge' consists of various components: clearly episodic parts referring to specific situations with their concrete (local-temporal, etc.) features; clearly semantic parts with concepts and relations that are abstracted from such concrete situations; and gradual forms of mixing and blending like schemata of events and processes.

According to this juxtaposition of concrete-episodic and abstract-conceptual knowledge, a reflection of such models of storing knowledge and meaning-making with episodic knowledge becomes relevant '… as the primary form by which human experience is made meaningful. Narrative meaning is a cognitive process that organises human experiences into temporally meaningful episodes' (Polkinghorne, 1988, p. 1). The analysis of knowledge referring to situations and episodes becomes particularly relevant in this context.

### Different approaches in one method

In interviews, the parts of everyday knowledge mentioned so far are more or less explicitly approached. On the one hand, semi-structured interviews can include narratives (Kvale, 2007). Mishler (1986) has studied what happens when interviewees in semi-structured interviews start to narrate, how these narratives are treated and that they are suppressed rather than taken up. In narrative interviews (Flick, 2006a, chap. 14), interviewees often switch during a narrative to descriptions, argumentations and other non-narrative forms of presentation. In this method, such forms of presentation are intentional in the last (balancing) part of the interview; in the narrative main part they are rather deviations from the ideal. However, an approach of within-methods triangulation would suggest using both areas of knowledge systematically and a purposeful combination of approaches to both. According to such aims, the episodic interview was designed as a method to collect the components of everyday knowledge as outlined in Fig. 5.2.

The central element of this form of interview is that you recurrently ask the interviewee to present narratives of situations (e.g. 'If you look back, what was your first encounter with television? Could you please recount that situation for me?'). Also, you will mention chains of situations ('Please, could you recount how your day went yesterday, and where and when technology played a part in it?'). You will prepare an interview guide in order to orient the interview to the topical domains for which such a narrative is required. To familiarize the interviewee with this form of interview, its basic principle is first explained (e.g. 'In this interview, I will ask you repeatedly to recount situations in which you have had certain experiences with technology in general or with specific technologies'). A further aspect is the interviewee's imaginations of expected or feared changes ('Which developments do you expect in the area of computers in the near future? Please imagine, and tell me a situation that would make this evolution clear for me'). Such narrative incentives are complemented by questions in which you ask for the interviewee's subjective definitions ('What do you link to the

**Semantic Knowledge**

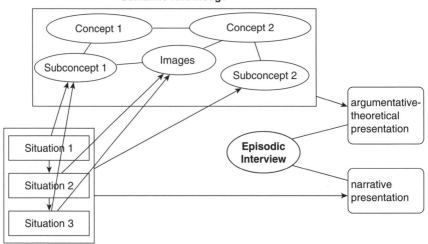

**Episodic Knowledge**

FIGURE 5.2    Areas of everyday knowledge in the episodic interview

word "television" today?'). Also, you will ask for abstractive relations ('In your opinion, who should be responsible for change due to technology, who is able to or should take the responsibility?'). This is the second large complex of questions aimed at accessing semantic parts of everyday knowledge.

### Concepts of health and ageing as an example

The principle and structure of the episodic interview will be demonstrated with the interview schedule for our study on professionals' health concepts (see Flick et al., 2003, 2004c), which includes three major components:

- Questions and narrative stimuli referring to the interviewee's health concept.
- Questions and narrative stimuli concerning health in old age.
- Questions and narrative stimuli referring to prevention and health promotion.

In this study, general practitioners and home-care nurses were interviewed. Health concepts were addressed with questions concerning doctors' and nurses' subjective concepts of health and their relevance for professional work and with narrative stimuli referring to them. It was instructive to see what were recounted as concrete situations, but also the selection taken from a wide host of descriptions of situations that would also have been possible. This shows the events causing health concepts to be developed or changed. We assumed that health concepts and practices change in the course of a life, as both have a biographical component and are modified by specific personal (e.g. illness) or professional experiences (with patients or resulting from further education). Furthermore, we were interested in links between subjective health concepts and practices and the professional handling of the issue. A background assumption here is that the issue of health allows it less than illness to keep a distance for oneself from professional work.

The second complex of questions and narrative stimuli focuses on health promotion. It aims at the professionals' understanding of this issue and at giving information about the part prevention and health promotion play in their day-to-day practices. This should reveal the relevance of health promotion in the professional routines of doctors and nurses. It should also show how far discussion of public health, prevention and health promotion have influenced medical and nursing practices.

The third complex addresses concepts of health in old age and the professionals' attitudes towards prevention and health promotion in their work with (very) old people. We also asked for the evaluation of one's own training and how much it helped in the later professional confrontation with health and old age.

Box 5.1 includes excerpts from the interview guide. Here, the narrative stimuli addressing episodic knowledge are labelled as E-1, etc.; questions addressing semantic knowledge are marked as S-2, etc. Using this interview guide leads to the presentation of the concept in form of a definition (in this case of health), as in the following example:

I: What is that for you, 'health'? What do you link with the word 'health'?

IP: With the word 'health', well quite a lot, not only free of illness, but a feeling well all around, to feel well mentally as well, to feel well socially, that means in the social frame you live and so on. ... Yes, one could maybe say also, free of financial concerns, what is surely part of it, because financial concerns make you ill, too.

---

**Box 5.1**  Example of an interview guide for an episodic interview

Concepts of health and ageing

*In this interview, I will repeatedly ask you to tell me situations in which you have had experiences with the issues of 'health' and 'ageing'.*

S-1  What is that for you, 'health'? What do you link with the word 'health'?

E-2  What has influenced your idea of health in particular? Can you please tell me an example that makes this clear for me?

E-3  Do you have the impression that your idea of health has changed in the course of your professional life? Please tell me a situation that makes this clear for me.

*(Continued)*

*(Continued)*

**E-4** Do you have the impression that the way you handle the issue of health has changed compared to earlier times? Can you please tell me an example that makes this clear for me?

**E-5** Do you have the feeling that your private practices referring to health influence your professional practice? Can you please tell me an example that makes this clear for me?

**E-6** What does it mean for you, to promote health in your professional practice? Can you please tell me an example that makes this clear for me?

**E-7** Have your professional practices changed in the last few years in what concerns the promotion of health? Can you please tell me an example that makes this clear for me?

**E-8** Would you please tell me how your day went yesterday? How, when and where did the promotion of health play a role in it?

**S-9** What does '(old) age' mean for you? What are your associations with that term?

**E-10** What role does 'age' play in your life? Could you please tell me a typical situation?

**E-11** When you think back, what was your most important experience with 'age' in your professional life? Could you please tell me a typical situation?

**E-12** Do you have the impression that your idea of age has changed in the course of your professional life? Please tell me a situation that makes this clear for me.

**E-13** What makes it clear for you, in your professional life, that a person is old? Could you please tell me an example of this?

**S-14** What does 'health in older age' mean for you?

**E-15** Do you have the impression that your professional training has prepared you sufficiently for the issues of 'health' and 'ageing'? Please tell me a situation that makes your impression clear for me.

**S-16** If you think of health promotion and prevention in your professional work, what relevance should they have for senior citizens?

**S-17** Was there anything in the interview that was missing for you or anything you found annoying?

On the other hand, the interviews provide narratives, for example about how changes were initiated:

**I:** What has influenced your idea of health in particular? Can you please tell me an example that makes this clear for me?

**IP:** There are actually very many examples. Well influenced, my personal opinion is simply influenced by the fact that our children, we have three children and the three big ones, when they were born, that was 19 and 18, 17 years ago, were both very sick. For our son, the older one, we did not know if he survived the first night. And then I had the feeling that a switch turned in me, yeah? Well was turned. Up to then, I need always a lot of formal security, local security, financial security, and that became completely unimportant for me from that day, when the decision was so much in the air. And at that time, I have started to develop my own relation to school medicine. I have traditional school medicine training and I have then started to organize many things in the family in another way first, by talking, by physiotherapy, by acupuncture, ozone/oxygen therapy. And as that worked quite will, I have applied it with patients, too.

Finally, we find mixtures of definitions and narratives of how the interviewee has developed this definition and what played a role in this:

I: What is that for you, 'health'? What do you link with the word 'health'?

IP: Health is relative, I think. Someone can be healthy, too, who is old and has a handicap and can feel healthy nevertheless. Well, in earlier times, before I came to work in the community, I always said, someone is healthy if he lives in a very well ordered household, where everything is correct and super-exact, and I would like to say, absolutely clean? But I learned better, when I started to work in the community. ... I was a nurse in the (name of the hospital) before that, in intensive care and arrived here with completely different ideas. And I had to learn that anyone should be accepted in his domesticity the way he is. And therefore, I think, health is – it always depends on how someone feels. Well, someone can have a disease, and feel healthy nevertheless. I think that's how it is.

## *Representations of technological change in everyday life as an example*

For the situations that are recounted in the episodic interview, we can distinguish several types, as the following examples from a study on the social representations of technological change may demonstrate (see Flick, 1996). First, we find that episodes – concrete situations, a specific event – that the interviewee has experienced, are recounted or mentioned:

I: When you remember, what was your first experience with technology? Could you please tell me that situation?

IP: Well, I can remember the day when I learned cycling, my parents put me on the bicycle, one of these small children's bikes, sent me off, it was not that long, that I went by myself, my father gave me

61

some push and let me off, and then I continued to ride until the parking lot ended and then I fell on my nose. ... I believe this is the first event I can remember.

A second type of situations consists of repisodes, that is, representations of repeated episodes (in the sense of Neisser, 1981), some situation that occurs repeatedly. One interviewee was asked for a situation making clear on what it depends when he watches television and recounted:

I:      Which role does TV play in your life today? Could you please tell me a situation that makes that clear for me?
IP:    Really, the only time when television has a certain relevance for me is New Year's Day, because I am so struck, that I can do nothing else but watch TV, well I have been doing this for years, spending New Year's Day in front of the TV ...

A third type is historical situations, referring to some specific event. One interviewee referred to Chernobyl when he was asked for his most relevant experience with technology:

I:      What was your most important experience or encounter with technology? Could you please tell me that situation?
IP:    Probably, well, the reactor catastrophe at Chernobyl, because that has intrigued rather decisively the lives of many people, that made it clear for me the first time how much one is at the mercy of technologies. ...

### Triangulation of data sorts in the episodic interview

In the episodic interview, the different types of questions aim at different sorts of data (narratives, argumentations, explication of concepts) in order to triangulate them. As in other interviews, the data produced in applying the method do not in every case and always meet the ideal concept of a 'situation narrative'. Applications have shown that in the episodic interview not only these types of situations are presented, but also different sorts of data:

* *situation narratives* on different levels of concreteness;
* *repisodes* as regularly occurring situations, no longer based on a clear local and temporal reference;
* *examples*, which are abstracted from concrete situations, and metaphors also ranging to clichés and stereotypes;
* the subjective *definitions* (of technology or health) explicitly asked for; and
* linked to them, *argumentative-theoretical statements*, e.g. explanations of concepts and their relations.

The episodic interview produces different sorts of data, which are located at different levels of concreteness and relation to the interviewee. It aims at social representations (see Flick, 1998; Moscovici, 1998) and thus a mixture of individual and social thinking and knowledge. In the episodic interview, moving back and forth between narratives of situations that the interviewees have experienced themselves and more general examples and illustrations, if they result from a narrative stimulus, is not seen as a loss of authenticity or validity (as in other forms of narrative interviews). Rather this complements the variety of data sorts making up social representations. Thus, episodic interviews may include the sorts of data represented in Fig. 5.3.

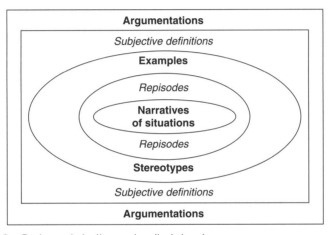

FIGURE 5.3    Data sorts in the episodic interview

The episodic interview is based on a triangulation on several of the levels that Denzin (1970) has suggested: different theoretical perspectives are linked to each other as well as the methodological approaches resulting from these perspectives, which then leads to different sorts of data.

## Examples of using within-methods triangulation

### Analyzing health concepts of health professionals

In what follows, an example of applying this strategy of within-methods triangulation will be outlined, which was mentioned before. The study 'Professionals' representations of health and ageing in home care for older people' (see Flick et al., 2003, 2004c) focuses on contents, relevance and, if applicable, changes in the concepts of health and ageing held by general practitioners and home-care nurses in two German cities. It should also inform about how far health as a leitmotif for professional practices has become part of the professional everyday knowledge of general practitioners and nurses.

The central research questions are:

- What is the specific concept of health in old age held by the professionals?
- Which dimensions of health representations are relevant for professional work with the elderly?
- What is the attitude of professionals towards health, prevention and health promotion for the elderly?
- What concepts of ageing do general practitioners and home-care nurses hold. What is the relation of these concepts with those of health?
- What is the relevance that is seen for one's own concepts of health and ageing for one's own professional practices?
- Are there links between the concepts of health and ageing and the professionals' training and professional experience?

Episodic interviews were conducted with 32 general practitioners and with 32 home-care nurses. In a short questionnaire, socio-demographic variables and structural data (training, professional experience, size of the institution, etc.) were collected. The analysis of the interviews shows that doctors' and nurses' health concepts are multi-dimensional, refer to somatic-mental well-being and are oriented towards the WHO definition – also in rejecting it in the case of some doctors. Both professional groups define health not only as the absence of illness, but see it as a continuum. This shows that the contents of Public Health and New Public Health have been adopted in the professionals' representations and their conceptual-semantic knowledge. At the same time, both professional groups do not only have a professional health concept. In the narratives of situations and examples, it becomes evident that health concepts are strongly influenced by personal and professional experiences in the confrontation with illness. Experiencing one's own illness and complaints has made them more understanding, emphatic and engaged in the work with patients. Their professional training has had for both groups no significant influence on their health concepts. For doctors as well as for nurses, it is evident that their concepts of health have changed as they have become more concrete and differentiated.

A change is not only described for the health concepts but also for private and professional practices referring to health. These changes are influenced by the private lives and by growing older on the part of the interviewees. The changes in professional practices referring to health have been initiated by moving from hospital work to home-care nursing in the case of the nurses. For doctors they were initiated by the limitations of medical treatments. As a consequence, both groups report a stronger integration of social and emotional aspects in treatment and care.

There are strong differences in how doctors and nurses describe their private practices with health. Many doctors present themselves as very aware of health, whereas nurses in the majority report that their practices are not really promoting their own health. This might be a reason why doctors confirm an influence of their private health practices on their professional practices, whereas nurses see private and professional life as separate in this respect.

## Analyzing health professionals' concepts of ageing

Concepts of ageing are mostly differentiated for doctors and nurses and comprise negative as well as positive aspects referring to the somatic, psychological and social life situation. Both professions' concepts refer almost exclusively to very old people. The representation of age moves to the group beyond 85 years old. It is interesting that hardly any positive body associations are mentioned. At the same time, we find certain indifferences in both groups' images of ageing, which is represented in their problems of defining age. Neither doctors nor nurses orient their definition of 'old age' at the calendar age. They mention subjective criteria for being old (e.g. mental and physical decline, amplification of certain negative traits), which are more deficit-oriented. Both groups mention numerous examples of patients who do not meet theses criteria; however, these people are not perceived as old. To some degree, age is seen as a signification of a form of living and of an attitude: 'You are as old as you feel and present yourself'.

Ageing plays a role in the doctors' and nurses' private lives, as both groups mention their own ageing as linked to restrictions and complaints or talk about older relatives. When asked for the most important experiences of age in professional life, doctors and nurses mention a number of positive examples of patients. Furthermore, they report experiences with death and dying. It is noticeable that the interviewees hardly draw any consequences from their experiences in private and professional lives and that they do not actively prepare for becoming old themselves.

Doctors and nurses describe a change in their images of being old that is initiated by personal or professional experiences. Furthermore, they talk of societal changes. These experience have made their images of age more multi-faceted and differentiated (see Walter et al., 2006).

Here we sometimes find significant differences between conceptual representations of health or ageing (at the level of conceptual-semantic knowledge) and the practices that are mentioned in examples and situation narratives (at the level of episodic-narrative knowledge), which become evident by triangulating both approaches (question/answer sequences and narratives). From the angle of quality in qualitative research, this strategy can provide different aspects of meaning, experience and relevance for the respondents and for the issue under study.

# Triangulation of different qualitative methods

Linking different research methods is the approach in triangulation that attracts most attention in qualitative research. On the one hand, this is embedded in a research approach – ethnography (see Chapter 6); on the other hand, this refers to combining qualitative and quantitative methods (see Chapter 7). Beyond that, more generally, this refers to combining different methods from different research approaches, but within qualitative research (see Fig. 5.4). This will be outlined next.

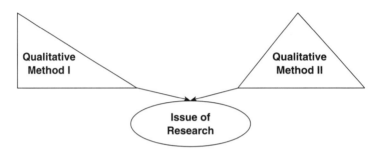

FIGURE 5.4   Triangulation of different qualitative methods

Here, we can again distinguish the use of triangulation for extending the knowledge of an issue or for mutually assessing results. In both cases, triangulation of different methods should start from different perspectives or at different levels:

> What is important is to choose at least one method which is specifically suited to exploring the structural aspects of the problem and at least one which can capture the essential elements of its meaning to those involved. (Fielding and Fielding, 1986, p. 34)

This can be realized by combining methods that focus on the – everyday, expert or biographical – knowledge of participants, with methods that are addressing the observable – individual or interactive – practices of members. If we take up this indication of triangulation, it does not make so much sense to combine two forms of interviews in one study, because they both may address different aspects of knowledge but will not go beyond the level of knowledge in collecting data. This would be the case if interviews were complemented by a method like observation or an analysis of interaction. Focus groups also use an extended interactive context for collecting data and thus are also methods operating at a different level than single interviews. The same is the case if we combine methods of analyzing visual materials with interviews. In these contexts, some of the problems that will be discussed later (see Chapters 7 and 8) arise: should the triangulation focus on the single case, should all cases be studied using the different methods or are two partial studies the better alternative, the results of which will be compared or combined later on? Likewise, the question arises whether both methodological approaches should be applied in parallel or one after the other. For example, should interviews be conducted between, after or before an observation?

# Examples of between-methods triangulation

## *Interviews and conversation analysis*

In what follows, the application of triangulating different qualitative methods will be outlined in two examples. For this purpose, a study mentioned before will be used as a first example. Here, counsellors' subjective theories of 'trust in counselling' were reconstructed and linked to their counselling practices. All in all, 15 counsellors – psychiatrists, psychologist and social workers – from socio-psychiatric services were included. The methodological overall strategy was oriented towards developing grounded theories in the field (according to Glaser and Strauss, 1967). A core aspect to be revealed in this strategy is the participants' knowledge of the phenomenon. Reconstructing the participants' subjective theories pursues this aim. The starting point is that people in everyday life – or in their professional practice – develop stocks of knowledge that are structured similarly to scientific theories. This knowledge is partly implicit, partly explicit. Research makes a subjective theory completely explicit by reconstructing it.

A second aspect that should be focused on in the discovery process was how trust is produced in counselling practices. This can be pursued in process analyses of consultations. They can also give information about the functionality of the subjective theories, as a form of expert knowledge, for practice and routines. A triangulation of both perspectives does not only have the aim of a mutual validation of their results. It should also catch the phenomenon under study in its complexity from different angles. If we want to reach this goal, the methodological approaches should be located at different ends of the range of qualitative methods. According to Fielding and Fielding (1986), such a triangulation should in one way focus on the meaning of the issue for the participants. This was the purpose of reconstructing counsellors' subjective theories. In the second way, the triangulation should analyze the structural aspects of the problem, that was pursued in (conversation) analyses of consultations.

Accordingly, this study triangulates two perspectives: on the one hand, a subjective intentional, reconstructive perspective looking for the meaning of a phenomenon (like trust) for the individuals in their (professional) practices; on the other hand, a structural-interactionist and interpretive perspective is taken, which focuses on structural aspects of a phenomenon like trust as part of social practices. Therefore, activities and statements are contextualized in social interaction patterns. They describe the processes in the organization of conversations, and how they can be understood from the outside, with the perspective of the interactive

**67**

process, and not from the inside with the perspective of the participant. Intentions and actions of the individual (counsellor or client) are seen as accounts that can be analyzed in the context of the process and of the common production of what is going on. This aim is pursued by analyzing consultations according to conversation analysis (see Rapley, 2007).

This systematic triangulation of perspectives was employed at two levels:

- First, at the level of the single case to answer the question if relations between a counsellor's subjective theory and a consultation he or she had had with a client can be found. This shows functionality and action-relevance of the single subjective theory for counselling in the examined context.
- Second, at the level of comparative analyses: comparative systematization of the course of counselling shows regularities. If subjective theories are to be functional for those forms of talk and counselling, they must contain representations of those regularities found in the different course of talk. In this way a set of categories can be developed out of one source of data (consultations), which can be used for interpreting the other source of data (subjective theories). Based on these findings, the entity of examples can be interpretively evaluated in the last step.

These methodological approaches are put into concrete terns as follows. Subjective theories are captured in a semi-structured interview. The interview guide focuses on various areas like the definition of trust, the relation of risk and control, strategies, information and a priori knowledge, reasons for trust, its importance for psychosocial work, institutional conditions, and so on. Among others, the questions in Box 5.2 were used for these purposes. The interviewee's statements are afterwards visualized, structured and communicatively validated – with him or her – by using the so-called structure-laying technique (according to Groeben, 1990). In the interview we find a statement like 'Trust is made more difficult if the contact with the client comes about in an urgent situation and the counsellor (as social worker) always has in mind to observe if any strange, suspicious facts appear because of which he or she has to present the client to the physician in the team'. From this, the excerpt of a subjective theory in Fig. 5.5 results.

---

**Box 5.2    Excerpts from the interview guide for reconstructing a subjective theory**

- Could you please tell me briefly what you relate to the term 'trust' if you think of your professional practice?
- Could you tell me what are the essential and the decisive features of trust between client and counsellor?

*(Continued)*

*(Continued)*

- There is a proverb, 'Trust is good, control is better'. If you think of your work and relations to clients, is this your attitude when you approach them?
- Can counsellors and clients reach their goals without trusting each other?
- Will they be ready to trust each other without a minimum of control?
- How do people who are ready to trust differ from people who are not willing to trust?
- Are there people who are more easily trusted than others? How do those trustworthy people differ from the others?
- Are there activities in your work that you can practise without trust between you and your client?
- If you think of the institution you work in, what are the factors that facilitate the development of trust between you and your clients? What are the factors that make it more difficult?
- Does the way people come to your institution influence the development of trust?
- Do you feel more responsible for a client if you see that he or she trusts you?

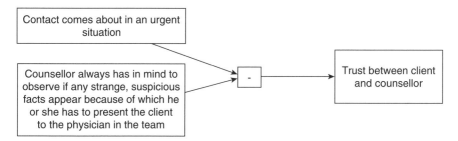

FIGURE 5.5   Excerpt from a subjective theory of trust

The second methodological approach in this study is to record (first) consultations that the counsellor interviewed before had with clients and to apply a conversation analysis to them. Analyzing the opening situation should reveal, first, how a situation of counselling is produced and how a relation of trust is built up with the client. This allows extrapolating developmental patterns of such situations and deviations from such patterns. The following extract documents the beginning of a consultation that was done by the social worker (B) just mentioned with a client (K):

→**B**:  Hmm, well, your grandfather came to us (K: yes), huh, he seemed to be very worried about you?
  **K**:  Yeah, I was feeling quite bad

**B**: Yes, what was the matter at that time?

**K**: In May, (.) you know, I drank too much a couple of days in a series and then I was feeling soo bad, because of the circulation (B: hmm), well everything, what you-, break out of sweat (B: hmm) raving of the heart, uuuh, burning eyes and everything, anyhow, and I didn't feel like laughing at all

→**B**: And then your grandfather also said, uh, well (.) your family doctor had said, meanwhile you are in a very urgent danger of death. Do you have an urgent organic-

**K**: Well, well, danger of death

**B**: complaints?

**K**: not really, ne? (B: hmm) There's just my fear, if I carry on that way, that still might come, (B: hmm) and that must not really happen, you know, I don't lay any stress on this (B: hmm) and therefore it's kind of a thing about drinking in my case.

**B**: How did it begin?

In the interventions marked by an arrow, the counsellor leaves the usual scheme – which could be shown across the consultations that were analyzed and also in similar studies before. According to this scheme, the consultation would start with exploring the problem from the client's point of view. In contrast to this, the counsellor first clarifies other aspects – the information she received from a third party (the grandfather). This deviation from the routine can be explained by the excerpt from the subjective theory in Fig. 5.5: the third party, the grandfather, gave hints that there is an acute situation with a possible endangerment for the client. The counsellor has to clarify this first in order to decide whether or not to present the client to the physician in the team. Only then can she start the consultation with the client in a traditional way and begin with the client's point of view ('How did it begin?') and build up a trustful relation.

In this example, the triangulation of both methods and of the data and results produced by both provides a complementary perspective at the level of the single case. In other examples, it provides divergent perspectives at this level. Divergent perspectives are particularly instructive as they raise new questions, for which we should seek theoretical or empirical answers (see also Flick, 1992, for this). Seen more generally, in comparing subjective theories, it could be shown beyond the single case how they represent the tasks and demands revealed by a comparative analysis of several consultations. Seen the other way around, a comparative analysis of the consultations shows the (for example, institutional) limitations of applying the subjective theories in professional practices.

### Interviews and focus groups

The second example is our study on professionals' concepts of health and ageing that was mentioned before. In addition to within-methods triangulation, different methods were also combined. Selected results from the single interviews were fed back and discussed in focus groups (see Barbour, 2007). These groups were organized in the two cities for the interviewed physicians and separately for the nurses. A main topic is the relevance of the health concepts we found for the participants' professional practices and a discussion of the consequences that should be drawn from them on how to plan these practices. The aim is to advance a transfer of the results into the health system and its practices. At the same time, new data are collected in these focus groups. Here, the stress is laid on the interactive aspect of collecting data: 'The hallmark of focus groups is the explicit use of the group interaction to produce data and insights that would be less accessible without the interaction found in a group' (Morgan, 1988, p. 12).

Focus groups are used as a stand-alone method or in combination with other methods (surveys, observations, single interviews, etc.). Morgan sees focus groups as useful for:

- orienting oneself to a new field;
- generating hypotheses based on informants' insights;
- evaluating different research sites or study populations;
- developing interview schedules and questionnaires;
- getting participants' interpretations of results from earlier studies (1988, p. 11).

In our study we pursued principally the last aim mentioned by Morgan. The general relevance of focus groups is characterized as follows:

> First, focus groups generate discussion, and so reveal both the meanings that people read into the discussion topic and how they negotiate those meanings. Second, focus groups generate diversity and difference, either within or between groups. (Lunt and Livingstone, 1996, p. 96)

In the focus groups, we could not feed back the whole range of our results from the interviews due to time and capacity reasons. As an entry into the discussion, we chose the barriers against prevention, health promotion and a stronger orientation towards health in the participants' own medical or nursing practice, which had been mentioned in the interviews. For all focus groups in this study, we planned a common concept of how to proceed, which was adapted to the number of participants and to the group dynamic in each case. For moderating the groups, we used the meta-plan technique. The groups should run though the following steps:

- *Entry.* In the beginning, the research project was briefly presented and the methods were described. Then selected results were presented that referred to the doctors' and nurses' attitudes towards prevention for older people and how to realize it.
- *Presentation of the barriers.* In the next step, we presented the barriers mentioned in the interviews on the side of the patients, of the professionals and of the health system. Sometimes, relatives (interfering with care and

**71**

making professional care impossible) and the surroundings (a missing elevator) have been perceived as barriers. In the focus of the following discussions were the barriers on the side of the patients and of the professionals.

- *Ranking.* After answering questions for a better understanding, we asked the participants of the focus groups to rank the barriers. By nominating the three barriers they individually felt to be the most important ones using meta-plan techniques, we produced a ranking for each group. This result was taken as a starting point for the following discussion of how to solve these problems.
- *Discussion.* As a stimulus for the discussion of the results, we used the questions 'Do you find your position represented in the result? What is missing for you?' The discussion about solutions to the problems mentioned here was initiated with the question 'Do you have any suggestions for how to overcome the barriers?'
- *Result.* At the end of the session, the main results of the discussion were noted on meta-plan cards, documented as a commonly produced result on a flip chart and finally validated with the group.

Focus groups as an additional methodological step allowed the participants to evaluate, comment and criticize the results from the interviews. This produced additional results at a different level – group interaction instead of single interviews. In addition to interviews and focus groups, other materials (curricula and journals) were analyzed in the study.

## Triangulating methods in qualitative research in the context of quality promotion

Within-methods triangulation aims at a systematic combination of different approaches in the context of one method. Its background should be the combination of different theoretical approaches. Its result will be the existence and connection of different sorts of data. Data triangulation according to Denzin may refer to using different existing data. Within-methods triangulation can be used for different purposes. In our examples, the central aim was to use the knowledge potential of two approaches systematically and to complement or extend them mutually. This should open up complementary perspectives on the issue in the experiences of the interviewees: a concrete process perspective, revealed in narratives of situations (when I first used the computer), etc. is complemented by an abstract description of a state (for me, a computer is …). This allows showing different facets of how interviewees subjectively deal with an issue. Thus, at the abstract level of general relations, a female French information engineer repeatedly argued about the gendered barriers for women of approaching a computer or technologies in general. In the concrete situations, she recounted a consistent success story of how she mastered resistant machines and complicated situations.

Within-methods triangulation, as the examples should have shown, is given when different approaches in one method are used systematically and are theoretically well founded. A pragmatic inclusion of open questions in a questionnaire consisting of closed questions is not a typical example for within-methods triangulation, nor is the acceptance of narrations in an interview, which is generally based on question/answer sequences.

The triangulation of different qualitative methods makes sense, if the methodological approaches that are combined open up different perspectives (e.g. knowledge and practices), introduce a new dimension (e.g. group interaction versus. single interview), start from different levels (e.g. analyzing documents or images versus. verbal data) or if the potential gain of knowledge is systematically extended compared to the single method. Additional knowledge can be used for confirming (validating) the results coming from one method. Even more instructive will be methodological triangulation, if it provides complementary results, that is, a broader, more comprehensive or even complete image of the issue under study. Particularly challenging are divergent results coming from different methods demanding additional theoretical or empirical explanation. Thus, methodological triangulation makes different contributions to quality promotion. It can provide a fuller picture of one issue (what do people think of something and how do they act referring to it?), it allows comparing the results of different approaches (do people act as they say they do or as they think one should do?) and it can extend the levels at which an issue is studied (knowledge, practice, institutional background). All these contributions can be made if different methodological approaches coming from qualitative research are combined explicitly in one method or by linking several methods.

A specific extension of within-methods triangulation in qualitative research will be discussed in the following chapter, where the triangulation of different approaches within the research strategy of ethnography will be discussed. A special version of between-methods triangulation will be discussed in Chapter 7, where combinations of qualitative and quantitative research will be the issue.

## ▭▭▭ Key points

- Triangulation can be applied within qualitative methods and between them.
- In both cases it allows combining different perspectives on an issue in one research design.
- This will produce different sorts of data, which can be analyzed per se or with respect to the promotion of quality.

## Further reading

Triangulation of qualitative methods is the issue of these texts:

Denzin, N.K. (1989) *The Research Act* (3rd edn). Englewood Cliffs, NJ: Prentice-Hall.

Fielding, N.G. and Fielding, J.L. (1986) *Linking Data.* Beverly Hills, CA: Sage.

Flick, U. (2000a) 'Episodic interviewing', in M. Bauer and G. Gaskell (eds), *Qualitative Researching with Text, Image and Sound: A Handbook.* London: Sage, pp. 75–92.

# 6
# Triangulation in ethnography

**Chapter objectives**
After reading this chapter, you should know

- that ethnography as a research strategy often comes close to the idea that using several methods contributes to the quality of a study;
- that triangulation in ethnography is often used implicitly, but that there are also ways of using it explicitly in the field; and
- that here again triangulation contributes to quality by combining different perspectives on one issue rather than by a pragmatic combination of methods.

Whereas the preceding chapter dealt with triangulation in or between qualitative methods (like interviewing), we now come to a field where implicit and explicit triangulation of methods has been seen as a feature of good research for some time, without always making the link to the promotion of quality in qualitative research sufficiently clear. In what follows, we will address the use of triangulation in ethnography from the angle of quality promotion.

## From participant observation to ethnography

Ethnography as a research strategy (see Angrosino, 2007; Atkinson et al., 2001) has increasingly replaced participant observation (see Lüders, 2004b, p. 222) – at least in what concerns the methodological discussion. For participant observation, Denzin has already mentioned the triangulation of different methods as a feature: 'Participant observation will be defined as a field strategy that simultaneously combines document analysis, interviewing of respondents and informants, direct participation and observation, and introspection' (1989, pp. 157–8). Accordingly, we find a number of works in the literature about qualitative research in the 1960s and 1970s that are devoted to the combination, differences and relative strengths and weaknesses of participant observation and interviews as part of it; see, for example, Becker and Geer (1960) but also Spradley's (1979) suggestions for the ethnographic interview, and more generally, the studies of Glaser and Strauss (1967).

For some time, triangulation has attracted special attention in the methodological discussion in ethnographic research. Marotzki (1998, p. 52) mentions the combination of participant observation and interviews as typical of Malinowski's research. The Marienthal study of Jahoda et al. (1933/1971) combined several (qualitative and quantitative) methods in an ethnography without mentioning the term triangulation explicitly. For more recent educational ethnography, Marotzki (1998, p. 47) sees the triangulation of methods and of data sorts as the rule, whereas a methodological discussion about it remains rather cautious. Methodological triangulation has become relevant for ethnography in general. Lüders (1995, p. 32) sees ethnography developing into a research strategy that includes all possible and ethically legitimate options of collecting data.

In this context, Hammersley and Atkinson's considerations are of special relevance: 'Data-source triangulation involves the comparison of data relating to the same phenomenon but deriving from different phases of fieldwork, different points of respondent validation, the accounts of different participants (including the ethnographer) involved in the setting' (1983, p. 198). Beyond triangulating data sources and different researchers, they mention 'technique triangulation' as a third form. Their aim in this is to use the comparison of data collected using different methods for controlling the 'validity threats' that are inherent in every technique: 'Here, data produced by different techniques are compared. To the extent that these techniques involve different kinds of validity threat, they provide a basis for triangulation' (1983, p. 199). This understanding of triangulation seems to be strongly informed by a technique orientation and claims for validation, as is underlined here:

> Ethnography often involves a combination of techniques and thus it may be possible to check construct validity by examining data relating to the same construct from participant observation, interviewing, and documents. ... What is involved in triangulation is not the combination of different kinds of data per se, but rather an attempt to relate different sorts of data in such a way as to counteract various possible threats to the validity of our analysis. (1983, p. 199)

Hammersley continues to use such a concept of triangulation, which emphasizes a validation perspective, in more recent publications (1996, p. 167). At the same time, Hammersley and Atkinson discuss several problems linked to such a concept. They emphasize that in data triangulation it is not possible to combine different data per se (Hammersley and Atkinson, 1983, p. 199). Rather, a relation between the data is constructed in such a way that we counteract the validity threats. They also emphasize that it is less the convergence than the divergence of data sorts that is instructive. According to this understanding, in comparing a person's knowledge and practices, triangulation should aim less at finding confirmation that the person acts according to his or her knowledge analyzed before. Rather it should focus on the question of how to explain discrepancies between knowledge and practices theoretically. That is why Hammersley and Atkinson call their approach 'reflexive triangulation' (1983, p. 200).

## Implicit triangulation in ethnography: hybrid methodologies

Methodological approaches that are necessary for realizing the aims of a study are triangulated in ethnography, even if the term triangulation is not always explicitly used. At the end, we often have not only a mutual validation of results coming from single methods but an extension of the knowledge potentials about the life world under study. As the different methods like observation and interviewing are mostly combined ad hoc in a situation of prolonged participation, we can also talk of an implicit triangulation in ethnography. Characteristic of ethnographic research is the flexible use of different methodological approaches according to the situation and the issue in each case. Not only is the use of the methods adapted to the situation, but perhaps also the methods themselves (Lüders, 2004b, p. 226). Already Hammersley and Atkinson have stated this: 'The ethnographer participates, overtly or covertly, in people's daily lives for an extended period of time, watching what happens, listening to what is said, asking questions; in fact collecting whatever data are available to throw light on the issues with which he or she is concerned' (1983, p. 2). In more recent publications as well, it is especially this flexible use of all possible sources of information as data that is suggested for ethnography, without explicitly spelling out the combination of specific methods or a formalized combination of specific sorts of data: 'One must engage in what Denzin called triangulation, checking everything, getting multiple documentation, getting multiple *kinds* of documentation, so that evidence does not rely on a single voice, so that data can become embedded in their contexts, so that data can be compared' (Deegan, 2001, p. 34).

For Amann and Hirschauer (1997, p. 19) ethnography is characterized by a – compared to other qualitative research strategies much stronger – methodological imperative of the field over the discipline (methods, theories, etc.). They want to make clear that it is not the preferences for specific methods resulting from a certain disciplinary tradition or discussion – for example in sociology – that should determine the researchers' encounter with the field under study (and with the empirical 'material'), but the methodological needs that are produced by the field, its features and peculiarities. For the 'data materials' produced in such encounters, Amann and Hirschauer state:

> Diverse documents are collected and produced: those produced by the participants (artefacts, divers writings), interview documents, recordings of conversations, video clips. Such documents can mutually interpret and control each other in a data corpus. Even if only single skimming procedures from such a list are used, it is their embedding in the context of an enduring participant observation which makes them ethnography. (1997, p. 16)

With such a characterization of the data in ethnographic research, the authors come rather close to the concept of data triangulation. For collecting this variety of data, they state, 'The decisive methodological step for establishing an empirical ethnography is the liberation from those methodological constraints that impede the immediate, personal contact to social events' (1997, p. 17).

If we look at the research practices that have been published according to this conception – for example in the collection by Hirschauer and Amann (1997) – it becomes evident that this liberation from methodological constraints refers to three points: in entering the field, in deciding which concrete methodological approaches to take to the interesting practices and members, and in how rigorously the methods are applied. Narrations are often part of the data, but not necessarily as a result of consequently applying narrative methods. But nevertheless, ethnographers use methods and normally a variety of methods (mostly observation, recording, interpretation and interviewing) in combination. Accordingly, Knoblauch (2004, p. 356) speaks of ethnography as being particularly predestined for 'hybrid methodologies' – the use of complementary methods addressing different aspects of issues. What is practised in such a hybrid methodology is nothing else than a concept of methodological triangulation, which goes beyond the idea of correcting and validating. However, it remains implicit as not much attention is paid to a systematic combination of methods.

## Explicit triangulation in ethnography: the precept of triangulation

Beyond such a pragmatic or implicit use of triangulation in ethnography, we also find a growing discussion of explicitly combining specific methodological approaches. Some authors (like Marotzki, 1998, and Schütze, 1994), even talk of a precept of triangulation:

> This means for me the honest commitment to combine different methods of data collection and analysis, different data sorts and theories according to the research question and area in such a methodologically controlled way, that a research design results that allows to provide credible and reliable knowledge about the person in his or her socio-cultural context. (Marotzki, 1998, p. 52)

For Marotzki this precept of triangulation refers to the combination of participant observation and interview technique or, for Schütze (1994), to the combination of narrative interviews and analyses of protocols and documents of interaction processes. Schütze sees ethnographic reports, original texts, narratives, and expert interviews and focus groups as sorts of materials for ethnographic research: 'As these sorts of materials have different references to realities, and as in ethnography, "holistic" phenomena should be recorded, in which very different perspectives on realities are involved, in ethnographic research data sorts and methods triangulation is normally indicated' (Schütze, 1994, p. 235).

For Schütze, this precept of triangulation above all is relevant in the context of using ethnographic research and results as a starting point for training (in social work) and consultation of clients (by social workers). But Schütze does not request the precept of triangulation without restrictions: 'A truly ethnographic study is not content with a structural description of one sort of material and with its symbolic interpretation, whenever the collection and inspection of several sorts of materials is viable and justifiable' (Schütze, 1994, p. 247).

Practical considerations of resources and impositions for participants or fields are mentioned here. A critical discussion of the concept and application of triangulation in ethnography comes from Kelle (2001). She breaks down an abstract methodological discussion of triangulation to concrete questions of research practice in ethnography. First of all she underlines that methods cannot be taken offhand out of the research perspective in their background: 'Various procedures cannot ... be thought and brought together at arbitrary parts of the research process, but only applied in parallel' (2001, p. 193). Then she highlights that junior scientists often carry out the research projects. They 'have to acquire theories and methodological tools not infrequently in the course of such a project'. Therefore 'using several methods cannot per se be seen as better than concentrating on one methodological procedure' (2001, p. 193).

For the first point of her critique, it could be noted that the approach of a systematic triangulation of perspectives (see Chapter 4) addresses this question. Here, the aim is not the simple combination of methods at arbitrary parts of the research process but the combination of methods by taking into account the theoretical methodological research program from which they come. The second point Kelle makes addresses the precept of triangulation formulated by Schütze and Marotzki, which raises the question of when a triangulation is indicated (see Chapter 10 for this).

More instructive is Kelle's approach to discussing questions of triangulation of research perspectives for concrete problems of collecting and documenting research materials. Kelle discusses these questions against the background of combining participant observations (documented in observation protocols) and interaction practices (documented in audio or video recordings). The background of her discussion is the distinction between reconstructive and interpretive methods (Bergmann, 1985; see also Chapter 4). In this distinction, a quasi-genuine access to the reality under study is attributed to the latter, whereas the former is attributed a (re-)constructive filter. As Kelle shows, both forms of documentation are characterized by selective filters. In one form, the subjective condensations of the observer or in producing the field notes are the origin of the filter. In the other form, the limited reach of the recording machines in time, in focus and in what can later still be transcribed is the reason, especially when the medium of recording lacks selectivity in what is recorded. More generally, Kelle demonstrates that any form of collecting and communicating data is a constructive effort and that no method allows a genuine access to what is studied. According to Kelle, any method produces reductions in the complexity of what is under study, but she holds at the same time: 'These reductions are necessary, if you want to be able at all to make a specific statement about the area of research, because it is not possible to put all aspects of a complex practice "under the microscope" at the same time' (2001, p. 202).

Kelle provides good arguments for a reflexive approach to triangulation in ethnography. She proposes to reflect the possibility of linking methods at the level of the concrete application and especially at the level of the forms of documentation necessary for each method. This is an important suggestion in the discussion of triangulation in general. The same is the case for her advice that an application of different methods needs a profound knowledge and training in each of these methods. However, it is less convincing to turn this argument against using triangulation in general. In another paper (Dausien and Kelle, 2003), she argues for combining ethnographic and biographic perspectives and expects that 'considering the biographicity of social interaction ... leads to thicker ethnographic descriptions and analyses' and that 'the methodological consideration of the situatedness of practical intersubjective sense-making in interactions beyond interview situations may enlarge the perspectives of biographical research' (Dausien and Kelle, 2003, pp. 1–2).

In summary, such approaches of explicit triangulation in ethnography outline ways to complement the limitation of ethnography – the here and now of what can be observed – by enlarging the perspective beyond situations of observation into a biographical framework or more generally to knowledge used by the participants in the observed situations.

## An example of triangulation in ethnography

80    As an example of using triangulation in ethnographic research, a study of the processes of building communities in traditional and new sports will be used

(Gebauer et al., 2004). For this study, several fields were selected in which the sport practices in traditional sport (handball as a team sport in clubs), in new forms of sport (inline hockey in public places) and in mixtures and combinations (triathlon), and their social representations (Flick, 1998; Moscovici, 1998), were analyzed empirically. Explicit triangulation was used here, as ethnographic methods of an extended participation and observation (see Angrosino, 2007) in the field, where new sports like inline hockey were played, were combined with the use of episodic interviews with single participants in additional appointments outside the observation. The first approach enables the researchers to analyze practices and communications. The second illustrates the meaning of the sport and the scene for the individuals.

The most consistent way is to apply the triangulated methods to the same cases (see Chapter 8). Persons observed in a field are (all) interviewed. This allows a case-oriented analysis of both sorts of data and to compare and link the different methodological perspectives for the single case. In addition, comparisons and links can be established at a higher level also. Patterns resulting from comparisons in one sort of data (process patterns of play in sports) can be linked to patterns coming from the other data form (emphases and blind spots coming up in all interviews in one field or in general). Sampling decisions have to be taken only once, as for both sorts of data the same selection of cases is used.

The disadvantages are that the load for an individual participant in the study is relatively high; to participate in observation and to give an interview is more than is usually expected from participants in a study. At the same time, the danger of dropout rises, as everyone who refuses either the interview or the observation is 'lost' for the whole study. Finally, observation in open spaces (like sport 'scenes' such as inline hockey on a town square) is confronted with the problem that perhaps so many persons are observed at the same time that not all of them can be interviewed, without going beyond the resources of the study. Therefore, triangulation again is possible only in a very limited way for the single case, but it can also start from the level of data sets.

Then the single methods are applied independently in the first step and produce a set of observational data and a series of interviews. Both are analyzed for their commonalities and differences. Triangulation refers practically to the results of both analyses and puts them into relation. As a practical problem, the question arises of how to ensure the comparability of the samples to which the different methods were applied.

Methodological triangulation in our example was oriented on three research perspectives:

1   Analyzing practices, interactions, codes, artefacts and gadgets, and forms of movement in different forms of organizing games in each sport.
2   Analyzing social representations of each sport.
3   A sociological analysis of social localizations and memberships.

## Triangulation of methods

The following methods were triangulated: ethnographic participant observations and descriptions of the field of each sport; episodic interviews with the members focusing on representations of the sport and of their own and group-specific practices; and a questionnaire focusing on the social background and affinities for localizing the members in the social sphere.

Ethnographic participant observation was understood as a research strategy (according to Lüders, 2004b) for analyzing concrete contexts and human development in a cultural surrounding (Jessor et al., 1996). A special interest was developed for clothing, rituals and symbols, which are used for marking social territories. Ethnographic participant observation can be used for analyzing social frames (Goffmann, 1974) by capturing aspects of space, time, noise (music, signals), objects and devices, rules, norms, codifications, and so on. Research questions in this study focused on social organizations and memberships in the single field. Are members more oriented towards trainers or role models or more on peer groups? Does the sport support individualization or not? Which performative acts, self-presentations and movements are typical for each form of sport? Which codes, rituals and symbols are used to indicate members in the community of each sport? (see Angrosino, 2007).

## Phases of observation

In making ethnographic participant observation work, we can distinguish three phases (according to Spradley, 1980, p. 34): (1) Descriptive observation in the beginning is for the orientation in the field and provides unspecific descriptions. It is used to grasp the complexity of the field as comprehensively as possible and to develop more focused research questions and perspectives. (2) In focused observation, the perspective is increasingly narrowed to the processes and problems that are particularly relevant for the research question, whereas (3) selective observation towards the end is more intended to find further evidence and examples for what was found in the second step, such as types of practices or processes. Particularly for the second and third phases, an observation manual was developed with key aspects like description of space, structure of time, contents of training, descriptions of persons, ways and structures of communication, level of body and gestures, rules, norms and habits.

## Structure of observational protocols

The resulting protocols of observation had the following structure: day, date, period of observation; name(s) of observer(s); keyword for the main event; situation of arrival; list of events in keywords; chronological description of the observations; description of conversations; the researchers' own feelings and reflections of their activities in the field; first interpretations, question, hypotheses; and open questions and hypotheses for the next observation.

One problem in ethnographic participant observation is often how to limit and select situations of observation in which the phenomenon under study becomes 'visible'. That is why more or less comprehensive interviews with participants are often used. In our case, triathlon can be mainly localized for the swimming training in a way that (a group of) athletes can be systematically observed. The other activities (running, cycling) are hardly accessible for observation, as they are practised by single actors and not at defined places. Such activities are better accessible in interviews.

## Episodic interviews in sports

Accordingly we did episodic interviews in this study, in which question/answer sequences were triangulated with narratives. With the first questions, the interviewees were invited to explain their subjective definition of the issue of research, for example: 'What is the meaning of triathlon for you? What do you link to the word "triathlon"? What characterizes the atmosphere of triathlon for you? Could you please tell me a situation that makes that clear for me? Could you please try to remember the situation in which you decided to do triathlon as a sport and tell me that situation?' Instructive for the analysis is the concrete situation, which is narrated in what is reported as happening in it, but also the selection taken from the multitude of possible situations for elucidating one's viewpoint. The next step is to clarify the role or relevance of the issue for the interviewee's everyday life. For this purpose, interviewees are asked to tell a typical daily routine in order to highlight the sport's relevance in it ('Please tell me how your day went yesterday and where and when triathlon played a role in it'). The interviewer can pick up certain aspects for probing from this multitude of situations. In the next step, the interviewees are asked to explain their personal relation to central aspects of the research issue for their life in general, for example: 'What is the role of sport in your professional life, your professional education? Could you please tell me a situation for this?' In the end, interviewees are asked to talk about more general aspects of the issue and to unfold their personal views ('On what does it depend, if someone decides for this sport and continues to do it? Could you please give me an example of this?'). This aims at extending the perspective. As far as possible, the interviewer should try to link the general statements with the interviewee's personal and concrete examples in order to let possible contradictions and discrepancies become visible. As in other interviews, interviewees should be given the chance to add something they felt was missing in the interview at the end.

The episodic interviews for all the sports in this study included narrative stimuli and questions for the following areas: subjective meaning of the sport; relevance of the sport in everyday life; social affinity or distinction through this sport; and a final, evaluative part (see Chapter 5).

The empirical material for interpretation, which resulted from both methodological approaches, included on the one hand case studies for single actors based on interviewing them and field descriptions for the fields under study, and on the other hand, more general analyses on the basis of the empirical material (see Gebauer et al., 2004). In what follows, short excerpts from a field description and from a case study will be presented.

### Triathlon as a field

In Berlin, we find about 1000 people organized in triathlon clubs. Triathlon competitions have been organized here since the middle of the 1980s, so triathlon is a rather young form of sport. In the competitions we observed, the relation between male and female participants was consistently around 3 to 1. It was interesting that the men, who started in five-year classes, were dominated by the 35–45-year-olds. The actors themselves classified triathlon mainly as a higher-level sport and clearly dissociated themselves from popular sports such as handball and above all soccer. In triathlon, in contrast to many conventional club sports, which are concentrated on an architectonic, specifically designed, special space like a gym or a stadium, we have to speak of spaces (using the plural) of this sport. Already the different spaces where triathlon is practised demonstrate its position as a hybrid between traditional and post-conventional sport. In indoor swimming pools, the swimming training is held at fixed times, often together with members of swimming clubs and under their organisational regimen. Diverse and continuously newly defined tracks for cycling and running at the edge of town are cycled individually or in small groups.

The triathlon meetings and competitions take place in special places. Only the swimming pools and the locations of the competitions are accessible for an ethnographic observation. Only here do the athletes gather and only here does the culture of the ethnicity under study constitute in a locally concrete way. Only here does the field 'triathlon' have clear physical and local boundaries. In other words, triathlon is not only a transgression at the levels of achievement and time limits, but also a local extension of traditional sport practices. In some sense, the sport practices start in the swimming pool, at a clearly defined location, in order to burst out beyond the boundaries and to transgress them. The practice of triathlon reproduces in itself the changes from conventional sport, which is limited and tied to specific local ghettos and fixed times, to post-conventional sport practices, for which it is constitutive to burst these limitations and to claim spaces for sport practices that have so far been spared out of this.

In triathlon, the swimming training is the 'fixed point, where you always meet', as one female participant states. Here, the athletes meet at fixed hours of training. They are locally put together, but they are seldom amongst themselves, but mostly with other club swimmers and – during the public hours – with leisure swimmers. In order to work against a possible mix-up with ordinary swimmers, the athletes distinguish themselves here again with their outward appearance (short, often blond-dyed hair, often tattoos, men's legs being shaved, everyone is wearing a noticeable watch) and behaviour: extended exercises of stretching and warming up, training schedules that are displayed beside the pool and consulted after each course, often only ephemeral hellos and goodbyes, and finally the – very individually operated – long periods of training.

In an observation protocol, the researcher noted accordingly:

> Most athletes in triathlon seem indeed – as was announced by the trainer beforehand – to be concentrated very strongly on themselves. In the indoor pool, there was hardly any contact among them. What about the greeting and farewell sequences, what happens in the dressing rooms? During my observation, I had the feeling that they are not irritated at all to be observed by a stranger. My feeling of distance, or dissociation, seemed to be 'reproduced' in the relation between the athletes and to the trainer. The athletes act as a community of individualists already in the indoor swimming pool.

Competitions are central to triathlon. Only here can the athletes pass the swimming cycling and running courses in an immediate sequence, which are practised separately in the training. This requires special locations. Their regular use has to be restricted during the competitions. Therefore, triathlon competitions have to be registered with the police and other agencies. Streets have to be closed to traffic. Bicycle stands, changing facilities, organization and catering stands have to be erected. Triathlon practices do not integrate in the everyday forms of using public spaces, as for example inline hockey does. Rather they transfer such spaces into special areas for sport for a short time (and with problems and organizational effort). For the participants, competitions have the character of special events. Here, the community of the athletes becomes visible to itself. Here, the single protagonists meet. At these special locations and mostly at exceptional times (often very early on Sundays) they can experience themselves as a community. At the competitions, the athletes – together with trainers, family members and friends – are their own audience. External spectators would be, as a protagonist puts it, 'bored to death' by such competitions, because the proceeding in the competitions, the athletes' fights against themselves and their rivals can be displayed to viewers only with difficulty.

To compensate for this performance deficit, which is constitutive for triathlon, bigger competitions of nationwide interest are produced as events with an extended supporting program. The athletes appreciate such events for their special atmosphere; they accept long journeys, expensive hotels and high fees for being part of the triathlon at Ratzeburg or the 'Iron Man' at Roth in Germany. Triathlon as a field has formal organizational structures of clubs and associations in common with traditional sport. However, the explicitly instrumental relation of the athletes to such organizational forms is characteristic for triathlon. Often membership is only seen as relevant for having access to and the opportunity of training in the indoor pools. Many athletes only use the swimming training in the context of the club and practice the other two disciplines (cycling and running) by themselves or – if the individual schedules can be coordinated – with a training partner. In contrast to most sport in clubs, competitions are seldom run as competitions between clubs or club teams. Rather it is the individual competition in well-differentiated age groups defined by the association that is central. The instrumental relation to and individualist erosion of the social form of the club in triathlon become most evident in the missing of all those festivities and meetings that are typical for sport clubs and that serve to cultivate and maintain sociability. For such a club life beyond the sporting practice, often the localities like club houses, regularly frequented pubs, and so on, are missing in triathlon. Protagonists who have taken over voluntary club positions repeatedly complain about the missing sociality of the athletes. The other members continuously state that the club, beyond the functional aspects mentioned before, 'actually does not have any relevance for the contacts among us', as one participant in our study puts it.

### Subjective meaning of triathlon

Observation and field descriptions allow revealing practices and social relations that are characteristic for the field. The subjective meaning of the sport and the individual representations of community linked to this sport are more accessible in the narratives in an interview. Therefore, some excerpts from the analysis of an interview with a female protagonist from the field of triathlon will be presented next. At the time of the interview, the interviewee is 27 years old and looks back on an almost lifelong career in sports: 'I began as a six, seven year old with track and field … I was drawn in by a family who all do track and field. … ' Across many steps she finally arrived from athletics to triathlon, which she had practised for three years 'properly', that is, training every day, regular participation in competitions and in club structures, in which she invests a lot of energy: 'Well, I am not a high-level athlete in a strict sense but upper mass sports section, I would say.' It is noticeable in this interview that the interviewee – in contrast to other interviewees – hardly mentions any positive aspects of this sport and its protagonists in her description of triathlon. She describes the athletes as obstinate, rigid single fighters, who are 'not open' and 'often not so funny and happy'. They permanently ignore themselves and their own feelings and prove incapable of building up more intense, mutual social relations. According to her description, it is not the ones looking for the particular, intense and extravagant who practise triathlon but only those who cannot help doing it. Thus the membership in this sport is based less on a selection and decision, which could always be revised again ('There are never such people who completely stop and start again. Such people feel the inclination again, well a friend of mine, she thinks, well somehow it was quite a nice time, but she'd never start again'). Rather it is based on a personal trait of the protagonists: 'Either the people are athletes from their personal type, I'd say, and then they stop for a little while and then continue. … ' The negative stylization starts with refusing the Greek and seemingly antique word creation 'triathlon' and the pretension it transports: '… before I started to say: "I do triathlon", I have actually always said, when asked, what sport I do, it almost was the case today, although I have been doing triathlon for two three years, that I said, well, I run, cycle and swim. But this triathlon per se has a strange meaning, somehow, … well for me this a little strange concept.' In a emphatically prosaic understatement, she prefers her sport to be understood as 'running, cycling and swimming'; she does not like to use the strange label 'triathlon', which aims at distinctiveness and exclusivity.

In the further development of the interview, mainly two related aspects are the grounds for her negative image of triathlon and of the athletes linked to this sport. For her, athletes are characterized by 'not much knowing themselves, never doing anything according to their feelings … they permanently ignore themselves'. The self-discipline invested by the protagonists for managing the enormous stint of training in triathlon ('You have often to convince yourself extremely and you need quite a lot of self-discipline for this sport') has a flavour of masochism for the interviewee. The athletes debar themselves from traditional pleasures and lust, in order to obtain satisfaction from a sometimes extreme 'self-torture'. This masochist relation to oneself even becomes evident in the way in which the 'athlete per se' uses a sauna:

> … you sit in the sauna, actually sauna should be something nice and relaxing, and the last time I suddenly recognized, I came into the sauna, I thought, I fall backwards out through the door again. This guy had turned it to 100 degrees (Celsius), sits and scrubs himself with a horse brush, and I think, that's unbelievable. The more the better, the more torture the better. …

The interviewee's presentation of these self-techniques, which are characterized by discipline, rigidity and escalation, includes an ambiguity that is rooted in the second core aspect of the negative image of triathlon she outlines: although the athletes permanently ignore themselves, they are permanently concerned with their own interests in an almost pathological self-centredness. This extreme self-centredness, which permanently misses the own self, obstructs any reference to others. They are 'amazingly individualistic … everyone works for him or herself', they 'do their own thing … and it does not matter for them, whether you are there or not'. As mentioned before, they are 'not open' and therefore not only unable to integrate into a community built on solidarity and reciprocity, they are also unable to have an intense love relationship:

I mean, that has something to do with a relation, and that is of course not found by persons who need, let's say, so much warmth and cordiality and much affection. Well, this is expressed rather extremely now, but I think that in particular athletes then again have fewer problems in their relationships, which one actually expects, because the people who are in such a relation are not so demanding in the wish of being together.

This presentation shows a polarity that gives a contour to the interviewee's negative stylization of triathlon (and the athletes) against the background of her own self- and world images. In her critique of the individualism of athletes, it becomes evident that she (as a sports club activist in particular) much appreciates orientations towards communities, cohesion and solidarity. In contrast to a life planned for the sport, in which rigid daily training programs dominate every other activity, she draws a positive image of features and states like being relaxed, easy-going, all in all a nonchalant laissez-faire. This includes sometimes saying: 'Today, I don't feel like it, I'll lie in bed and watch TV' or 'to have a nice breakfast and see what the day will bring'. Only at the very end of the interview does she outline a positive aspect of her triathlon practice; however, it remains unclear whether this is a wish or a real experience of hers:

And that so often what I miss so much. I often go to the training, because I think, well today the sun is shining, I am really keen now on driving around and watching the birds and simply to get out of the city and to rush along the forest cart roads and not because the training schedule says 90 minutes cycling now. And that is what I miss so often at the athletes, to look a little more at, what do I really want myself, yeah? That's all actually.

### Triangulation of observation and interviewing

The triangulation of both approaches in ethnography shows, first, how the distinction in the field is put to practice in activities, attributes and forms of communication, as the situation in the indoor swimming pool shows. Furthermore, the role of formal processes of community building and of individualizing and informal forms of dissociation as practices in the field in constituting social relations and communities become visible. This reveals the social construction of community in this field. The ambivalences that are linked to this form of (missing) community for the actors and the biographical pathways that have led them there are only (exclusively or complementarily) revealed in the interview. Here, the contribution of the individual to the social construction of the field shines through. This reveals not only commonalities in the data and analyses resulting from both methodological approaches, but even more the discrepancies and different facets that become possible only after the triangulation of methods and research perspectives outlined here.

# Triangulation in ethnography in the context of managing quality in qualitative research

Triangulation in ethnography is applied in varying forms and consistencies. At some points it is seen as constitutive for the ethnographic attitude in the field, but is then applied mostly implicitly. At other points it is explicitly and consistently requested even in a precept of triangulation. Problems that are raised refer to the necessary skills for applying two (or more) methods. Thus, Kelle ends her paper with a sort of scepticism: 'In the methodological literature, it is often pretended that one could make use of different theoretical approaches and methods as if they were ready on the shelf' (2001, p. 206). Successful use of triangulation requires a high, degree of theoretical skills and calls for working into the different approaches to be triangulated. But is that not the case for how ethnographic research practice has been described by authors like Lüders, Atkinson, Hammersley, Deegan or Angrosino anyway, even if the claim for triangulation is not made explicit? In ethnographic research practice, triangulation of data sorts and methods and of theoretical perspectives leads to extended knowledge potentials, which are fed by the convergences, and even more by the divergences, they produce.

As in other areas of qualitative research, triangulation in ethnography is a way of promoting quality of research. Often it is used in a more implicit than explicit way. It is even more important than in other areas, as in ethnography quality issues are treated implicitly less than in qualitative research in general. As one indicator of this, we do not find a chapter addressing quality issues per se in the otherwise excellent handbook of Atkinson et al. (2001). Good ethnographies are characterized by flexible and hybrid use of different ways of collecting data and by a prolonged engagement in the field. As in other areas of qualitative research, triangulation can help to reveal different perspectives on one issue in research such as knowledge about and practices with a specific issue. Thus, triangulation is again a way to promote quality of qualitative research in ethnography also and more generally a productive approach to managing quality in qualitative research.

## Key points

- Triangulation can be used in ethnography as a strategy for promoting quality of research.
- As issues of quality in general remain rather unspecific and are mainly linked to attitudes more than to explicit strategies in ethnography, the use of triangulation often remains implicit here also.
- Using triangulation in ethnography more explicitly can make the issue of quality promotion in ethnography more explicit also.

## Further reading

These authors address ethnography from the angle of using different methods in the framework of this approach and at the same time give an interesting access to ethnography as such:

Angrosino, M. (2007) *Doing Ethnographic and Observational Research* (Book 3 of *The SAGE Qualitative Research Kit*). London: Sage.

Deegan, M.J. (2001) 'The Chicago School of ethnography', in P. Atkinson, A. Coffey, S. Delamont, J. Lofland and L. Lofland (eds), *Handbook of Ethnography*. London: Sage, pp. 11–25.

Flick, U. (2007) *Designing Qualitative Research* (Book 1 of *The SAGE Qualitative Research Kit*). London: Sage.

Hammersley, M. and Atkinson, P. (1983) *Ethnography: Principles in Practice.* London: Tavistock (2nd edn 1995, Routledge).

Lüders, C. (2004b) 'Field observation and ethnography', in U. Flick, E. von Kardorff and I. Steinke (eds), *A Companion to Qualitative Research.* London: Sage, pp. 222–30.

# 7
# Triangulation of qualitative and quantitative research

**Chapter objectives**
After reading this chapter, you should understand

- how and when a triangulation with quantitative research can be used for quality promotion in qualitative research;
- that here in particular a simple combination of methods tends to neglect the methodological and often theoretical differences among both approaches;
- that a careful and successful triangulation of both approaches can be planned at several levels with different outcomes; and
- that quality in qualitative research can be promoted by integrating quantitative parts in the research not only at the level of quality assessment but also by adding more and different aspects of knowledge about the issue of research from each of the approaches.

The idea that quantitative research can be used to advance the quality of qualitative research is still and again in the air. It has become prominent again in particular in the context of discussions about mixed methodologies (Tashakkori and Tedlie, 2003a) and about all sorts of evidence-based practices (see also Morse et al., 2001, or Denzin and Lincoln, 2005, for this). Both discussions have a critical potential for qualitative research, as they tend to question the independence and value of qualitative research on its own. Despite this, a reflected use of quantitative approaches can contribute to the quality of research mainly or in part based on qualitative research. For taking up this suggestion, it seems necessary to outline how such a combination can be realized, which pitfalls and strategies should be taken into account in such a combination. Methodological discussions were marked for a long time by argumentations of sharp distinction, which highlighted the differences in the theoretical, epistemological and research practical starting points of qualitative and quantitative research. In the US discussion, this was even labelled as 'paradigm wars' (Lincoln and Guba, 1985). This distinction argumentation has led to sharpening the methodological profile of qualitative research and to a growing diversification in the field. It has also had the consequence that quantitative standardized research was relatively unimpressed and has pursued its topics and internal methodological issues. Both research areas – qualitative und quantitative research – have remained and developed relatively independently and side by side.

## The relevance of linking qualitative and quantitative research

Several trends in how to overcome a strict separation of qualitative and quantitative research can be noticed. A starting point is the notion, slowly being accepted, 'that qualitative and quantitative methods should be viewed as complementary rather than as rival camps' (Jick, 1983, p. 135). Such trends aim at linking qualitative and quantitative research. Following Bryman (2004), we can more generally distinguish two levels at which the relation of qualitative and quantitative research – and thus an option for or the impossibility of their triangulation – is discussed. At the level of 'epistemology', rather the fundamental incommensurateness of both approaches is focused, sometimes referring to the specific paradigms in each case. In the 'technical version' of the discussion, these differences are seen but not as impossible to overcome or to take into account. The focus is rather on the usefulness and contribution of one approach for the other. In a similar way, Hammersley (1996, pp. 167–8) distinguishes three forms of linking qualitative and quantitative research: *Triangulation* of both approaches stresses the mutual validation of results and not so much the mutual addition of knowledge potentials. *Facilitation* highlights the supporting function of the other approach in each case; for example, one approach provides hypotheses and ideas for carrying on the analysis with the other approach. And finally, both approaches can be combined as *complementary* research strategies.

Bryman (1992) identifies eleven ways of integrating quantitative and qualitative research. The logic of triangulation (1) means for him to check for example qualitative against quantitative results. Qualitative research can support quantitative research (2) and vice versa (3); both are combined in or provide a more general picture of the issue under study (4). Structural features are analyzed with quantitative methods and processual aspects with qualitative approaches (5). The perspective of the researchers drives quantitative approaches, while qualitative research emphasizes the viewpoints of the subjective (6). According to Bryman, the problem of generality (7) can be solved for qualitative research by adding quantitative findings, whereas qualitative findings (8) may facilitate the interpretation of relationships between variables in quantitative data sets. The relationship between micro- and macro-levels in a substantial area (9) can be clarified by combining qualitative and quantitative research, which can be appropriate in different stages of the research process (10). Finally, there are hybrid forms (11), for example the use of qualitative research in quasi-experimental designs (see Bryman, 1992, pp. 59–61).

All in all, this classification represents a broad range of variants. (5), (6) and (7) are determined by the idea that qualitative research captures other aspects than quantitative research and that a combination is based on their distinctiveness. Theoretical considerations are not very prominent in these variants, as the focus is more on research pragmatics.

Beyond that, we often find the integration of qualitative and quantitative methods or mixed methodologies (Tashakkori and Teddlie, 2003a) and triangulation (Kelle and Erzberger, 2004) as concepts for linking both approaches. Which label is chosen in each case shows the different claims linked to each approach. Mixed methodologies are interested in facilitating a pragmatic combination of qualitative and quantitative research, which is intended to end the paradigm wars. Tashakkori and Teddlie (2003b, p. ix) declare this approach to be a 'third methodological movement', quantitative methods being the first and qualitative methods the second movement. A methodological elaboration of this approach is aiming at the clarification of concepts ('nomenclature'), of designs and applications of mixed methodology research and questions of inference in it. Using the paradigm concept in this context, two more or less closed approaches are assumed, which again can be differentiated, combined or rejected, without diving into the concrete methodological problems of linking both approaches. The concept of triangulation is rejected by several of the authors (e.g. Sandelowski, 2003; Tashakkori and Teddlie, 2003c), not least for pushing their own concept of mixed methodology research. Claims linked to mixed methodology research are outlined as follows:

We proposed that a truly mixed approach methodology (a) would incorporate multiple approaches in all stages of the study (i.e., problem identification, data collection, data analysis, and final inferences) and (b) would include a transformation of the data and their analysis through another approach. (Tashakkori and Teddlie, 2003b, p. xi)

These are very far-reaching claims, especially if we consider the transformation of data and analyses (qualitative in quantitative and vice versa).

This rather brief overview is intended to show in which contexts the combination of qualitative and quantitative approaches is currently being discussed. In what follows, I will try to spell out a little more what contribution can be expected here from triangulation as understood in our context.

## Qualitative and quantitative designs

In various contexts, the development of integrated designs comprising qualitative and quantitative research is discussed. Miles and Huberman (1994, p. 41) suggest four basic designs (see Fig. 7.1).

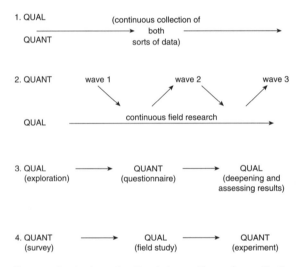

FIGURE 7.1    Research designs for the integration of qualitative and quantitative research (adapted from Miles and Huberman, 1994, p. 41)

### *Parallel use of qualitative and quantitative research*

In the first design, qualitative and quantitative are used in parallel. In the second design, a continuous field observation provides a basis for different waves of surveying. The third design starts with collecting qualitative data (e.g. in a semi-structured interview), which is followed by a survey as an intermediary step, before the results from both steps are elaborated and validated in a second qualitative phase. In the fourth design, a field study complements and deepens the survey results from the second step, which is followed by an experimental intervention in the field for checking the results from both steps (see Patton, 1980, for similar suggestions of mixed designs).

## Sequential combination of qualitative and quantitative research

Without necessarily reducing one approach to being inferior or defining the other as the main research, a study may include qualitative and quantitative approaches in different phases of the research process. Barton and Lazarsfeld (1955), for example, suggest using qualitative research for developing hypotheses that will afterwards be tested by quantitative approaches. Therefore, these authors are repeatedly taken as a starting point for defining a subordinate, only exploratory role for qualitative research or for dissociating one's own position from such an understanding. However, in their argumentation, Barton and Lazarsfeld do not focus only on the limits of qualitative research (compared to quantitative), but they explicitly see the strength of qualitative research in the exploration of the phenomenon under study. Following this argumentation, qualitative and quantitative research are located at different stages of the research process. These authors discuss explicitly various strengths of qualitative research, which they see in the discovery of relevant problems for research, in providing hints of phenomena that cannot be directly observed, in constructing descriptive systems, preliminary classifications and systematic typologies.

Exploring an issue under study is one of several functions of qualitative research. Even if Barton and Lazarsfeld (1955) see most of the functions of qualitative research they discuss as localized 'before quantitative research', the former is seen as a necessary precondition of quantitative research and less as a preliminary step, which can basically be left out also. Rather, Barton and Lazarsfeld discuss a series of examples to show that certain insights cannot be found or adequately analyzed without qualitative methods. According to them, qualitative research can reveal possible connections, reasons, effects and even the dynamics of social processes, and it is only qualitative research with an unstructured collection of data that can reveal this. At the same time, they see the innovative part of the research beyond tables of a few variables defined in advance and in qualitative data collection. Following their argumentation, qualitative and quantitative research are localized in different phases of the research process. Qualitative research should be positioned more at the beginning of dealing with an issue, but can also be used for the interpretation and clarification of results from statistical analyses. Thus, Barton and Lazarsfeld make suggestions for linking both approaches, which are similar to what Bryman (1992) proposed more recently.

## Mixed methodology designs of qualitative and quantitative research

In his systematization of research designs in qualitative and quantitative research, Creswell (2003) also refers to integrated designs and distinguishes three forms: (1) Phase designs, in which qualitative and quantitative methods are applied separately one after the other, no matter in which sequence. Such designs can include two or more phases. (2) The second form is named 'dominant/less dominant' design and is mainly committed to one of the approaches and uses the other only marginally. (3) Mixed methodology designs link both approaches in all phases of the research process.

In the context of the mixed methodologies approach of Tashakkori and Teddlie (2003a), Creswell (2003) and Creswell et al. (2003) suggest a more elaborate version of designs linking qualitative and quantitative research. They see mixed methods designs as being a design in its own right in the social sciences (2003, p. 211) and use the following definition: 'A *mixed methods study* involves the collection or analysis of both quantitative and/or qualitative data in a single study in which the data are collected concurrently or sequentially, are given a priority, and involve the integration of the data at one or more stages in the process of research' (Creswell et al., 2003, p. 212).

Their matrix for determining a mixed methods design is an interesting suggestion (see Table 7.1). The authors use the term 'triangulation' in the context of a design named as 'concurrent triangulation'. According to the categories in Table 7.1, this is characterized by a parallel collection of qualitative and quantitative data (implementation). The priority is preferably equal, but can be with quantitative or qualitative data. Integration comes with the phase of interpretation of results or in analyzing the data. The theoretical perspective is perhaps explicit (2003, pp. 224, 229).

TABLE 7.1   Decision matrix for determining a mixed methods design

| Implementation | Priority | Integration | Theoretical perspective |
|---|---|---|---|
| No sequence concurrent | | At data collection | |
| Sequential – qualitative first | Equal | At data analysis | Explicit |
| Sequential – quantitative first | Qualitative | At data interpretation | Implicit |
| | Quantitative | With some combination | |

From Creswell et al. (2003), p. 218

96

## *Integrated longitudinal designs*

Kluge (2001) describes 'integrated panel designs', in which several waves of qualitative interviews and repeated quantitative surveys for one research question are combined in order to study changes in viewpoints and interpretive patterns of the participants: 'Particular in this methodological approach is not only the parallel use of qualitative and quantitative methods of collecting and analysing data, but also to link both methodological strings in a *longitudinal perspective*' (Kluge, 2001, p. 41). The aim here is first to test how far the qualitative results can be generalized by the quantitative results (2001, p. 41). At the same time, the first approach is seen to be addressing the actors' perspective, whereas the second studies social structures. Central for the methodological integration is to contribute to an integration of the results (2001, p. 44; see also Kelle and Erzberger, 2004): 'All in all, the integration of qualitative and quantitative procedures contributes to a bigger gain of knowledge. If the results are complementary … , a fuller picture results. If the results are convergent, they validate each other … And if they are contradictory, this may lead to more and important research' (Kluge, 2001, p. 44).

Research designs integrating qualitative and quantitative research methods can be classified according to the sequence of methodological approaches, to the weight given to each approach, their function, and according to the theoretical and methodological reflection of the combinations. Here we can distinguish the combination of methods for extending the knowledge potentials of research and for a unidirectional or mutual assessment of the results. A mutual addition in the methodological perspective on the research issue is assumed here. The addition comes from a complementary compensation of weaknesses and blind spots in the single methods. However, the different methods remain standing side by side, their point of intersection is the research issue. Whether the methods are used at the same time or one after the other is less relevant than that they are used on an equal footing in the project.

# Linking qualitative and quantitative methods

Triangulation can refer to linking different qualitative methods, as in ethnography (see chapter 6), but it is also relevant for linking qualitative and quantitative methods. Here as well, integrative approaches are discussed. Kluge (2001, pp. 63–6) describes four variants of integrating qualitative and quantitative methods of data collection:

1   Using the focusing of standardized surveys for designing an interview guide for interviews – in Kluge's examples the problem-centred interview of Witzel (2000) – and the orientation of the interviewing on these aspects.

2   To produce life-course charts, in which data about the life course of an interviewee from a survey are elaborated visually (according to a time axis), which can then be presented to the interviewee for comment.
3   Subjective views and interpretive patterns becoming visible in interviews are transformed into items of the subsequent standardized survey.
4   In interviews of the panel at a later date, questions are integrated that aim at clearing issues from the standardized survey, which is also mentioned as an example for a communicative validation (Kluge, 2001, p. 64).

For analyzing data, Kluge refers to the option of integrating quantitative data in the computer-assisted analysis of qualitative data (e.g. with ATLAS.ti or Nudist; see also Gibbs 2007) or to use interfaces to SPSS. Finally, she mentions quantitative techniques (cluster analysis) for analyzing qualitative data for developing typologies (2001, p. 74).

Brewer and Hunter (1989) have presented an approach of 'multi-method research'. They are interested in a 'synthesis of styles' and start from four basic methods of empirical research that can be combined in different ways. These basic methods are field research (the approach of Glaser and Strauss, 1967), surveys (using representative questionnaires), experimental methods and non-reactive measurements. As a leading concept, they use for combinations the triangulation with reference to Denzin (1970). However, they talk of 'triangulated measurement' in the logic of mutual validation of results (Brewer and Hunter, 1989, p. 17). They discuss their approach of triangulation or multi-method research in applying it to all phases of the research process. All in all, they cleave too much to the logic of standardized research, in which they simply want to integrate field research.

Johnson and Hunter (2003) pick up the question of linking qualitative and quantitative methods in the context of 'mixed methodologies', but do not develop specific approaches. A standard example used here again is to include open questions with free text answers in an otherwise standardized questionnaire. Seen the other way round, we can then also describe the documentation of quantitative information (like age, income, number of children, years of professional experience, etc.) or certain scales in an otherwise open interview as a form of integrating qualitative and quantitative methods of collecting data (see Flick, 2006a, chap. 22 for the use of documentation sheets for collecting such data in the context of episodic interviews). Finally, data analysis in both cases will include the linking of qualitative and quantitative approaches: in the first case the coding of the free text answers, in the second of the numbers received. More elaborate here is the use of time, speed and frequency rates in observations of movements and activities, as in the study of Jahoda et al. (1933/1971).

For analyzing qualitative data, Kuckartz (1995) describes a method of coding of first and second degree, in which dimensional analyses lead to defining variables and values that can be used for classifications and quantifications.

Roller et al. (1995) outline a method of 'hermeneutic-classificatory content analysis', which integrates ideas and procedures of objective hermeneutics (see Reichertz, 2004) in a mainly quantitative content analysis. In a similar direction goes the transfer of data, analyzed using programs like ATLAS.ti, into SPSS and statistical analyses. In these attempts, the relation between classification and interpretation remains rather fuzzy.

From a more general point of view we can conclude that in most cases one approach is dominated by the other and integrated in the latter in a more marginal way (for example, we often find a small number of open questions among a multitude of closed questions in a questionnaire), which is why these examples seldom represent a triangulation of qualitative and quantitative methods. The development of really integrated qualitative/quantitative methods remains a problem to be solved. Concrete suggestions of how to integrate both approaches in one method, which really could be called 'triangulation', are still awaited.

## Linking qualitative and quantitative data

Morgan (1998) suggests a classification of approaches of linking qualitative and quantitative research, referring mainly to the level of data collection. He organizes his classification first around the 'priority decision', that is, which method is in the foreground during data collection, which one is subordinate, and around the 'sequence decision', that is, which sequence is chosen here. This leads to the matrix in Fig. 7.2.

|  |  | Priority | |
|  |  | *Qualitative* | *Quantitative* |
|---|---|---|---|
| Sequence | **Preliminary** | M1 | M3 |
|  | Follow-Up | M3 | M4 |

FIGURE 7.2   Classification of linking qualitative and quantitative research in data collection (following Morgan, 1998; Bryman, 2004, p. 455)

Wilson (1981, pp. 43–4) has outlined a systematization of aspects that characterize social situations, with which they can be analyzed and which provide clues for selecting qualitative or quantitative methods and their combination. He distinguishes in this context 'the objectivity of social structure', existing independently of the actions of the individual and which influences actions via norms and rules. The 'reference to commonly shared stocks of knowledge' makes it possible to understand and localize the other and his or her action in the situation. The 'context-dependency of meaning' has its reason in the fact that the specific meaning of an

99

action or statement is different according to each specific context and can only be understood in this context. Here, we can distinguish two opposite approaches. On the one hand:

> The radical quantitative view focuses entirely on the experienced objectivity of social structure and transparency of displays, while treating the context-dependency of meaning as merely a technical nuisance to be dealt with in specific research situations but without theoretical or methodological relevance. ... In contrast the radical qualitative position emphasizes the context-dependency of meaning but neglects the objectivity of social structure and transparency of displays. (1981, pp. 43–4).

On the other hand, Wilson's classification can be taken as a starting point for a more comprehensive approach to social reality:

> The social world is constituted through situated actions produced in particular concrete situations and which are available to the participants for their own recognition, description and use as warranted grounds for further inference and action on those same occasions as well as subsequent ones. Situated actions are produced through context-free, context-sensitive mechanisms of social interaction, and social structure is used by members of society to render their actions in particular situations intelligible and coherent. In this process, social structure is both an essential resource for and a product of situated action, and social structure is reproduced as an objective reality that partly constrains action. It is through this reflexive relation between social structure and situated action that the transparency of displays is accomplished by exploiting the context-dependences of meaning. (1981, p. 54)

Another form of combining qualitative and quantitative research can be realized at the level of the data, when we transform the data from one strategy into the other – from qualitative into quantitative data and vice versa. In the programmatic of 'mixed methodology research' the transformation of one form of data into the other is advocated (see above), but without making concrete suggestions of how to do it.

### Transformation of qualitative data into quantitative data

Attempts to quantify statements in open or narrative interviews come up repeatedly. Observations can be analyzed in their frequency also. The frequencies with which categories are filled can be counted and the numbers in different categories can be compared. Counting specific features in transcripts or observation protocols can be a way to transform qualitative data from content analysis into nominal data, which can then be computed using statistical methods. Hopf (1982) criticizes a tendency in qualitative research to convince readers of research reports with argumentations based on a quantitative logic (e.g. five out of seven interviewees said, the majority of answers referred to) instead of looking for a theoretically based interpretation and presentation of results. The argumentative pattern criticized by Hopf can also be seen as an implicit transformation of qualitative data into quasi-quantitative results. In the course of this transformation, a de-contextualization of information is undertaken, for example when the frequency of a certain statement is isolated from the specific contexts in which it was done and regarded separately.

### Transformation of quantitative data into qualitative data

The inverse transformation normally is more difficult, as a re-contextualization of singular data would be necessary. From questionnaire data, the (meaning) context of the single answer can hardly be reconstructed without explicitly using additional methods, like complementary interviews with a part of the sample. While analyzing frequencies of certain answers from interviews can provide additional information for the interpretation of these interviews, we need new data sorts (interviews, field observations) to be collected and added to explain why certain patterns of answers come up more often in a survey.

## Linking qualitative and quantitative results

Links between qualitative and quantitative research are often established for the results that both have provided. Accordingly, Kelle and Erzberger (2004) focus in their more general works on linking qualitative and quantitative research mainly on the level of results. They distinguish three alternatives:

1   Results may converge, that is, are consistent completely, in general, by tendency or partially. For example, answers in a representative survey using standardized questionnaires converge with statements from semi-structured interviews with a part of the sample of the survey in one of the variants mentioned above.
2   Results may be complementary to each other. Then interviews provide complementary (deepening, detailing, explaining, extending, etc.) results in addition to what the analysis of the questionnaires has shown.
3   Finally, results may diverge, that is, in the interviews (completely, generally or partially) different views compared to the questionnaires come up. This would be the reason for further theoretical and/or empirical clarification of the divergence and its causes.

For all three alternatives, the same questions and problems come up in principle: How far was the specific background of both empirical approaches (in collection and

101

analysis) taken into account? Do divergences perhaps result from the different understanding of reality and issue in both (qualitative and quantitative) approaches? Should convergences to a (too) large extent not be the reason for being sceptical rather than a simple confirmation of one result by the other? Finally, how far are both approaches and their results seen as equally relevant and independent insights, so that using the concept of triangulation is justified in this concrete case? How far is one or the other approach reduced to a subordinate role, for example for only giving plausibility for the results of the other approach?

## Triangulation of qualitative and quantitative research in the context in quality assessment in quantitative research

Triangulation in the context of linking qualitative and quantitative research has been discussed with a strong focus on mutual assessment of the quality of research and results for a long time (e.g. Jick, 1983). For example, we can use qualitative research for assessing the validity of data produced with a standardized instrument, as the following example may show.

To ensure and produce (again) quality of life is especially important when people live with a chronic illness. Then it has to be assessed which form and extent of quality of life can be achieved with certain treatments. Accordingly, research into health-related quality of life (Guggenmoos-Holzmann et al., 1995) is booming. Internationally and in different language areas, quality of life indices such as the SF-36 (see Mallinson, 2002) are used. For this instrument, a claim to be a generally valid index for assessing health-related quality of life is made. For the validity of this and similar indices, several questions are discussed that are interesting for our context. Most of the scales used in these indices have been developed in the US. In transferring them to other language areas some validity problems become particularly visible, which arise in one cultural or language area if different populations with different cultural backgrounds inhabit it. Validity problems discussed in the context of quality of life indices are: How far can lists and items of physical and social functionality as included in quality of life indices be seen as equivalent to subjectively experienced quality of life? How far can they be transferred to the different social and local contexts in a society with the same validity? The item 'Are you able to walk five blocks every day?' may be an indicator for quality of life in American towns. In some areas of bigger cities, it rather indicates an overly venturesome behaviour. To translate into German 'five blocks' as a measure of the ability to move is quite difficult. Nevertheless, these items and scales are used for international comparison of the quality of life in different countries.

Mallinson (2002) studied for the SF-36 the limits of the unambiguousness of questions for the respondents. This can be shown in the commentaries noted by participants in studies of quality of life at the margins of the questionnaires. These showed that the participants sometimes understood the questions completely differently from what the developers of the instrument intended. With the SF-36 they want to find out how far respondents are restricted in certain everyday activities. For this they are asked, for example:

> The following questions are about activities you might do during a typical day. Does your health limit you in these activities? If so, how much? (Please circle one number on each line).

> **G**:  Walking more than a mile    Yes limited a lot, Yes limited a little, No, not limited at all
> **H**:  Walking half a mile    Yes limited a lot, Yes limited a little, No, not limited at all
> **I**:  Walking 100 yards    Yes limited a lot, Yes limited a little, No, not limited at all

Parallel open-ended interviews in Mallison's application of the SF-36 show that many participants in such studies have problems of getting straight in their minds how far one mile or half a mile or 100 yards is:

> **IV**:  Can you walk half a mile?
> **IE**:  Where's half a mile?
> **IV**:  Say down to the garden centre, maybe a little bit further than that.
> **IE**:  I can walk down to the garden centre, but there's no way I could get back because it's up-hill and as soon as I, I can't walk up that hill so it depends which, if you're talking about on the flat, slowly, not talking or carrying anything. ... (p. 16)

Beyond such validity problems of items and scales on the side of the questions that are asked, validity problems for the answers also arise. If the answer format is a Likert scale (very good; good; fair; poor; very poor; or in the example above: Yes limited a lot; Yes limited a little; No, not limited at all), we can ask furthermore whether the distance between the single gradations in different language is the same or not. This leads to the question of whether we can simply summarize or compare the circles around one of the alternatives without problems. In this example, triangulation of an open (qualitative) procedure with a standardized (quantitative) method shows the limits of validity for statements collected using the second method.

In the other direction, Silverman (1985, pp. 138–40) sees a way for assessing the generalization of qualitative results in adding quantifications. An alternative is the further contextualization of qualitative data by consulting quantitative data and an additional check of their plausibility. So our study of general practitioners' and nurses' health concepts showed that the interviewees hardly attributed any relevance to their professional training. Rather, professional experiences in their own practices and private experiences with health and illness are attributed the strongest influences. For contextualizing this result, we analyzed the curricula and training plans for the professional training of nurses and for medical sciences over a longer period for the quantitative relevance of topics like health, health promotion and prevention. In my study of counsellors' subjective concepts of trust in socio-psychiatric services in Berlin, it became evident that the dilemma between counselling and helping the client on the one hand and the administration of deviant behaviour on the other hand determines the problematic of building trustful relationships in a particular way. In addition, the – purely quantitative – documentation of interventions was analyzed over a longer period. This showed first a shift in the centre of the work from placements of mentally ill persons in psychiatric wards towards counselling as an intervention for psychological problems. However, they also showed how large the part of placements still is in the practices of the institutions. In these examples, quantitative data are used for contextualizing qualitative data and interpretations and to give them more plausibility.

## Examples of triangulation of qualitative and quantitative research

In what follows, some examples of triangulation of qualitative and quantitative research will be given.

### Coping with cancer in the family

Schönberger and Kardorff (2004) studied the challenges, burdens and achievements of cancer patients' relatives in a combination of a questionnaire study with two waves of surveys (189 and 148 relatives and 192 patients) and a number of case studies (17, of which 7 are presented in more detail). The research questions for both parts of the study were characterized as follows:

> On the background of the existing research, we have focused on the experience of burdens, on individual and partnership coping, on integration in networks and the evaluation of the services in the system of rehabilitation. The social scientific hermeneutic part of the study aimed at discovering structure-theoretical generalisations. (2004, p. 25)

In addition, the authors conducted 25 expert interviews in the hospitals involved in the study and 8 expert interviews in after-care institutions. The participants for the case studies were selected from the sample for the survey. The criteria for selecting a couple for a case study were that: 'The couples should share a flat, the partner should not suffer from a severe illness, and the ill partner should be in a rehabilitation clinic or after-care centre at the time of the first data collection' (p. 95). Furthermore, contrasting cases to this sample were included: people living by themselves, couples with both partners being ill, or cases in which the patient's partner had died more than a year ago (2004, p. 95).

The quantitative data were first analyzed using several factor analyses and then in relation to the research question. In the presentation of the questionnaire results, 'a link to the case studies is made, if their structural features match findings from the questionnaire' (p. 87) or if they show exceptions or a deviance. All in all, the authors highlight the gains of differentiation due to the combination of survey and case studies (2004, p. 201):

> Thus the case studies not only allow for a differentiation and a deeper understanding of the relatives' response patterns to the questionnaire. Their special relevance is, that analysing them made it possible to discover the links between subjective meaning-making (in the illness narratives), the decisions and coping strategies and styles which were reported and the latent meaning structures. Going beyond the psychological concepts of coping, it became clear that it was less the personality traits or single factors which make it easy or difficult to stabilise a critical life situation. Above all, the structural moments and the learned capacities to integrate the situational elements in one's own biography and in the one shared with the partner were important. (2004, p. 202)

This study can be seen as an example of combining qualitative and quantitative methods (and data), in which both approaches were applied consequently and in their own logic. They provide different aspects in the findings. The authors also show how the case studies can add substantial dimensions to the questionnaire study. Unfortunately, the authors do not refer to which findings from the questionnaires were helpful for understanding the single cases or what the relevance of the quantitative finding was for the qualitative results.

## Youth in survey and portraits

Another example is the Shell Youth Survey 2002 (Hurrelmann and Albert, 2002). Here, a representative survey of 2,515 adolescents between 12 and 25 years old using a standardized questionnaire is combined with more detailed or short portraits of 'committed' adolescents. The sampling of these is described as follows:

> We had two main criteria for selecting the interviewees. On the one hand, the commitment: we interviewed adolescents who are involved politically or in the society. On the other hand the use of the Internet: for all 20 adolescents, in some way the criterion 'involvement in or through the Internet' should apply. ... The adolescents we interviewed were between 16 and 25 years of age. (Picot and Willert, 2002, p. 226)

Here, the quantitative results provide the framework for the situation of adolescents in Germany at the time of the study, whereas the qualitative interviews provide insights into two specific areas – commitment and use of the Internet – which are deeper in two respects: First, for these areas in reference to the single cases that are portrayed. Second, the single cases have the function 'to present the views of the youth. … The adolescents shall here become visible as the subjects of the interview' (p. 221).

Here again, both approaches have their own functions and both are put consistently into practice and used according to their particularities. The cross-references between both approaches and their results, however, remain rather limited. Rather both results are presented complementarily and side by side.

## Triangulation of qualitative and quantitative research in the context of managing quality in qualitative research

Combinations of qualitative and quantitative research are used more and more often also in the context of assessing and promoting the quality of qualitative research. Some methodological questions of this use have not been answered in a satisfactory way. A series of approaches of combining both exist, in which sometimes the systematic or the methodological level is secondary to a pragmatics concerning research practices or concepts. Attempts to integrate both often lead to the use of one after the other (with different ways of sequencing), side by side (with different degrees of independence for both strategies) or a super- or subordination (in either way). Integration often concentrates on linking the results or on the level of research designs – a combinatory use of different methods with different degrees of reference to each other. Furthermore, the differences between both strategies continue to exist for assessing procedure, data and results. The question should be further discussed, how to take this into account in the combination of both strategies, and in particular when this combination is used for advancing the quality of research.

There are some guiding questions for assessing examples of combining qualitative and quantitative research (see also Flick, 2006a, chap. 3):

- Are both approaches given an equal weight (in the plan of the project, in the relevance of the results and in judging the quality of the research, for example)?
- Are both approaches just applied separately or are they really related to each other? For example, many studies use qualitative and quantitative methods rather independently and in the end the integration of both parts only refers to comparing the results of both.
- What is the logical relation of both? Are they only sequenced, and if so, how? Or are they really integrated in a multi-methods design?

- What are the criteria used for evaluating the research all in all? Is there domination of a traditional view of validation or are both forms of research evaluated by appropriate criteria?

If we take the issues mentioned in these guiding questions into account, triangulation of qualitative and quantitative research can contribute to promoting the quality of qualitative research. Like other strategies and approaches mentioned in this book, it is not the one and only way to go towards more quality in qualitative research and is by no means appropriate in every project. Here, even more than in the other examples, the question of indication of methods (see the final chapter of this book) needs particular attention.

## ▬▬ Key points

- Triangulation of qualitative and quantitative research is not per se a quality indicator for qualitative research, but under certain circumstances it can contribute to impraning quality.
- In these cases we should take the different perspectives on an issue into account in using both approaches.
- This will produce different sorts of data, which can be analyzed per se or with respect to the promotion of quality of qualitative (and of quantitative) research.

## Further reading

In these sources, the combination of qualitative and quantitative research is discussed without falling into euphoria for mixing methods on a pragmatic level, so that they can give insights for the discussion of using triangulation of qualitative and quantitative research in the context of quality issues for qualitative research:

Bryman, A. (1992) 'Quantitative and qualitative research: further reflections on their integration', in J. Brannen (ed.), *Mixing Methods: Quantitative and Qualitative Research*. Aldershot: Avebury, pp. 57–80.
Flick, U. (2006a) *An Introduction to Qualitative Research* (3rd edn). London: Sage, Chap. 3.
Kelle, U. and Erzberger, C. (2004) 'Quantitative and qualitative methods: no confrontation', in U. Flick, E. von Kardorff and I. Steinke (eds), *A Companion to Qualitative Research*. London: Sage, pp. 172–7.

# 8
# How to use triangulation for managing quality: practical issues

**Chapter objectives**
After reading this chapter, you should know about

- the practical problems of using triangulation for quality promotion in qualitative research;
- how to plan sampling and comparison in using triangulation; and
- where you can integrate triangulation in the research process.

In the preceding chapters, I have used several examples from studies in which one or the other variant of triangulation was applied for contributing to the quality of qualitative research at the level of combining different approaches and results. In what follows, some of the practical problems known from such applications will be taken up again. This time the focus will be on how to plan and use triangulation for managing quality in qualitative research.

## Special problems of access

Wolff (2004) describes the problems that can arise when entering a field of investigation, and discusses what we can learn from them and the possible solutions.

He makes clear that social research in general and qualitative research in particular come with impositions to the field under study and its members. Examples of such impositions are:

- making available time for conversations;
- partially giving up control of physical space;
- enduring embarrassment;
- facing up to communicative pressures (such as those that arise in narrative interviews);
- limiting one's own communicative needs (if they are subordinate to a semi-structured regime);
- accepting the questioning of what has always been taken for granted.

They should also display a wide range of their own activities, such as

- putting themselves in the researcher's position (in order to be able to provide data interesting to him/her);
- informing the researcher about situational relevancies;
- smoothing the researcher's path and suggesting competent interview partners;
- answering questions they have never put to themselves, the meaning of which is initially obscure;
- trusting the researcher without guarantees;
- explaining to themselves and others what the researcher and the project are aiming at;
- signalling that one is not disturbed, even though they know they are under scrutiny, and so on. (Wolff, 2004, pp. 195–6)

In studies using several methods, this imposition of research is intensified even more. On the one hand, the impositions are doubled by the use of two (or more) methods. One the other hand, the time needed for participating in the study grows (not only is an interview to be given, but also continuous observation or the recording of conversations are to be accepted, etc.). This relatively higher effort increases the danger that potential participants put off the researcher and are not available for the study. In my study on trust in counselling, I had to face the extra problem of a selective readiness: several of the counsellors whom I had approached according to theoretical sampling with good reasons, agreed to give an interview, but not to have a consultation with a client recorded for research purposes. Others had no problem with such a recording, but were not ready for an interview. Both can lead to a considerable loss of interesting or – in terms of sampling – relevant cases.

Another problem in this context is that in combining interviews with observations in open spaces (markets, train stations, etc.), it is sometimes not possible to include all the people who are frequenting these spaces systematically in the study and have **109** them interviewed and observed and to obtain some kind of informed consent about being studied from them.

## Design and sampling

### Triangulation in case studies

For the design of a study using triangulation, similar questions arise as for designs in qualitative research in general (see Flick, 2004, 2007). Triangulation can be used in the context of one of the basic designs in qualitative research. You can plan a case study using a variety of data sorts or different methods or theoretical approaches. Hildenbrand (1999) describes, for his approach to case reconstruction, how he studies families as cases and first produces protocols of observations, which are then complemented by conversations about the family history and the analysis of documents.

### Triangulation in comparative studies

Studies using triangulation can also be planned as comparative studies. For the possible forms of comparisons, there is a multitude of options located at various levels. First you can plan comparison across the cases at the level of the application of one method: what are the commonalities and differences in the knowledge of the various interviewees ($case_{1-N}$) or in the practices of different participants ($case_{1-N}$)? Furthermore, we can compare the results of comparisons across the cases from applying both methods: how are commonalities and differences of knowledge in relation to those of practices? And finally, we can draw comparisons of the cases for the convergences and divergences at the level of the single case: can we elaborate a typology of relations between knowledge and practices? (see Fig. 8.1).

| Method I | | Method II |
|---|---|---|
| $case_1$ | Comparison | $case_1$ |
| $case_2$ | Comparison | $case_2$ |
| ... | | ... |
| $case_N$ | Comparison | $case_N$ |
| Comparison $case_{1-N}$ | Comparison | Comparison $case_{1-N}$ |
| | Comparison | |

FIGURE 8.1   Dimensions of comparison in studies using triangulation

### Temporal sequencing of triangulation

As was already mentioned for the combination of qualitative and quantitative methods, different forms of triangulation can be used for (only) qualitative methods, but three alternatives can be planned in temporal respects. Several qualitative methods can be used in parallel: at the same time as observation, interviews are done or the interviewee is immediately asked to provide a consultation. Different methods can be used in sequence: first all interviews are done and then a period of observation follows (or recordings of consultations are collected) or vice versa. Finally, the methods can be applied in an interlaced way: first observation, then interviews, then observation again. Both strings of research can be referred to one another.

### Triangulation in cross-sectional and longitudinal studies

Most studies using triangulation are done as cross-sectional studies. The integrated panel design that Kluge (2001) has presented includes several waves of interviews and standardized surveys (see Chapter 7). This can be transferred to the combination of several qualitative methods. Then, people would be interviewed repeatedly during an extended period or observations are carried out for a longer period and interviews are conducted in between phases of observations. Beyond that there are few longitudinal studies in qualitative research (Lüders, 2004b); the approach is extended in its range (more methods) and in time dimensions (repeated application of the methods) and the research design becomes over-complex compared to the usual qualitative research project.

### Planning of resources

In calculating the resources (time, methodological skills, costs, etc.) for a study using triangulation, you should take into account that researchers should have experience with the different methods, either in every method or in a division of labour. Because of the complexity of calculating the organization and running, research needs much more than what Miles and Huberman (1994, p. 47) or Morse (1998) suggest as resources for the single steps of qualitative research (see also Flick, 2004, 2007).

Finally, we can transfer the question of the relation of the single methods from the discussion about linking qualitative and quantitative research. Are methods used on an equal footing or is one method placed over the other or subordinated, the primary or the secondary one?

### Sampling

From the research question, sampling strategies derive concrete goals as to which empirical 'units' should be in involved in the study. The range goes from rather abstract (for example, according to a statistical numerical model) strategies like random sampling to more concrete strategies, which are based more on the contents of the study (like theoretical sampling according to Glaser and Strauss, 1967; see also Chapter 4) or a variant of purposive sampling (according to Patton, 2002; see also Flick, 2006a, chap. 11). Referring to sampling in studies using tri-angulation, we can discuss mainly three aspects: (1) How to guarantee that a sampling strategy fitting each single method can also be put into practice in the context of triangulation? (2) Which options of an interlaced sampling make sense? (3) How can we take into account or bring together the different logics of sampling of different methods or approaches?

### One sampling strategy for different methods

In our study on concepts of health and ageing, a sample of doctors and nurses in two cities was constructed according to certain criteria (Flick et al., 2004, chap 3; Flick, 2007) and put into practice. In the focus groups, which were run more than a year later, in principle the same sample should have been used. However, a number of dropouts occurred. Some interviewees said right away that they were not interested in participating in one of the groups. Others had to cancel shortly before the date of the group. In analyzing the results of the group and even more in linking them to the interviews, such differences have to be taken into consideration.

### Interlaced sampling

Interlaced sampling means that cases or groups for the application of the second method are selected from the sample drawn for the first method. For example, from a sample for a survey, some cases are selected that make up the sample for open interviews. Against the background of the interviews with several counsellors a sample is drawn among them (according to theoretical sampling). The members of this sample are asked to provide the recording of a consultation for applying conversation analysis – the second method in the triangulation. From observing an open space on a playing field, single cases are selected for inter-views by using their social localization in the observed social fabric as the crite-rion. In all these examples, substantial criteria can be developed from one part of the study for selecting the cases for the second part (see the example on coping with cancer in Chapter 7).

### Different logics of sampling

Finally, it should be considered in the application of different methods whether they each call for different samples. For interviews, sampling will address people. In observations it is rather the situation that is in the focus of sampling. Thus, it will not necessarily be the same persons who have to be included in the observation as were selected for the interviews.

# Collection and interpretation of data

## *Influences on the subject*

In this respect, some of the points already mentioned above for design issues apply. You should at least take time effects into account. When the different (qualitative or quantitative) methods are applied one after the other, you should reflect on how to take the time between data collections with both methods into consideration. In our study on health and ageing concepts, more than a year elapsed between the (first) interviews and the focus groups. In the meantime, the issue to be mentioned in the interviews and focus groups may have changed considerably – in this case, for example, due to health political discussions in the media, professional organizations, or in legal terms or political planning. Accordingly we should think about how far the participants in the interviews and later in the focus groups still talk about 'the same' and how to reflect those developments in the data and their interpretation.

## *Interferences between different methods*

A second aspect is the interferences of the different methods of data collection. In triangulating quantitative and qualitative methods, for example questionnaires and interviews, the relatively strong structure in the research situation in the standardized questionnaire may produce or confirm specific expectations towards research, which may radiate into the second research situation, so that the more open flow in narratives or the interview dialogue may be influenced by expectations for more structure. This may have the consequence that it will be more difficult to effectively use the strengths of the interview – its open structure – than it would have been without using a standardized method before. Similar influences are possible the other way round.

We should think about how to deal with knowledge from the other data collection. What the researchers know about the participants' knowledge from the interviews may lead them to just look for confirmatory (or contradictary) practices or events in the observation. This becomes relevant if we want to use triangulation with the focus on assessing the quality of the interview data and analysis (or of one method with the other), but also with the focus on consequently exploiting the full epistemological potential of each method.

Such interferences can be used purposively if researchers orient themselves in questions in an interview on what they learned from observations beforehand and focus directly on specific points in relation to them. Also, statements and results from interviews can be used to focus later observations more strongly. In a similar way, we deliberately used statements from the interviews before to stimulate the discussion in the focus groups with doctors or nurses in our health and ageing project.

113

In both cases it is essential to deal with such interferences in a reflected way, which means to clarify how to use or perhaps avoid them and to do this for every single case in a comparable way.

### Interpretation

In analyzing the different (sorts of) data coming up in a study using triangulation, the point just made for data collection can be further elaborated. Here, we can think of different strategies of linking the data. Each set of data can be analyzed separately: First, all interviews are compared in order to derive commonalities and tendencies. Then all observations are analyzed in a comparative way. Commonalities and tendencies are referred to the results from analyzing the interviews and vice versa.

Both sorts of data can also be referred to each other at the level of the single case and then analyzed. Finally, we can develop categories for the second set of data from analyzing the first one. From analyzing consultations, we can develop a general process model of consultation in the specific context under study. The phases of counselling that become evident here, come with specific 'tasks' for the counsellor in building a trustful relationship with the client. At the beginning of the conversation a relationship has to be established, a problem has to be identified, named and explored, and the clients have to be given enough space for unfolding their views of their problems. From these tasks, we can derive categories for analyzing the subjective theories of the counsellors that have been reconstructed in previous interviews. These categories can be useful for showing how far such phases and tasks are represented in the counsellors' knowledge in reference to how to put them into practice or in an idealizing way.

For within-methods triangulation, it may be useful to analyze the different sorts of data separately and in a contrasting way. For example, we can contrast the contents of narratives with those of subjective definitions. The question then is, for example, which commonalities and differences can be shown between nurses' subjective concepts of prevention and what they tell about how to put concepts of prevention into practice in their day-to-day work.

## Levels of linking qualitative and quantitative research

In triangulating qualitative and quantitative research, the question arises as to which level the triangulation concretely addresses. Here we have two alternatives. Triangulation of qualitative and quantitative research can be applied to the single case. The same persons who are interviewed are also members of the sample who fill in a questionnaire. Their answers to questions in both methods are compared, brought together and related to each other at the level of the single case as well. Sampling decisions are taken in two steps. The same cases are selected for both parts of the study, but in a second step it is decided which of the participants are selected for an interview. The link can be established in addition – or only – at the level of data sets. The answers to the questionnaire are analyzed in their frequency and distribution over the whole sample. The answers to the interview are analyzed and compared and a typology is developed. Then the distribution of answers from the questionnaire is linked to the typology and compared with it (see Fig. 8.2). This can be discussed in a similar way for combining two qualitative methods.

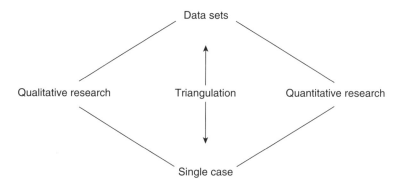

FIGURE 8.2    Levels of triangulation of qualitative and quantitative research

## Computers in studies using triangulation

### QDA software

In the meantime, not only for quantitative data, for which SPSS has become a standard software, but also for qualitative data, a number of software programs are available, mostly QDA (qualitative data analysis) programs (see also Gibbs, 2007, for more details). These programs are designed for supporting the analysis of textual data (interviews, conversation transcripts) and visual material (images, film, video). The most important programs are ATLAS.ti, Nudist, EnVivo, WinMax and MaxQDA (see Gibbs, 2007, for details). In contrast to SPSS they do not perform the analysis or the analytical steps themselves but they support the administration of texts or images and the retrieval and coding of material. Thus they are more like a word processor than a statistics program. For applying such programs in the context of a study using triangulation, we can discuss several problems.

### Administration of and links between different sets of data

In using different sorts of data (e.g. interviews and focus groups), we face the problem of how to administer them. In the ATLAS.ti program, for example, hermeneutic units are built for an analysis. They include the primary texts (the data) and secondary texts (memos, codes, networks of codes, texts written during the analysis, etc.). These are linked among each other and can be administered and processed in connected ways. The program does not care, of course, whether the primary data are of one sort (interviews) or different sorts of data (interviews and focus group transcripts). However, they should be labelled specifically so that it will be possible later on to see whether a statement comes from an interview or from a focus group. If both parts of the study are analyzed separately first, it may be useful to set up different hermeneutic units for each of the parts to avoid the files becoming too big. It has proved difficult to merge several hermeneutic units. Therefore you should consider handling all the data (sorts) in one such unit right away, especially in studies triangulating methods for data collection. For within-methods triangulation for example, for the episodic interview – the question may arise of how to code the various sorts of data (narratives and interviews) in a formal way to represent their distinctiveness. In programs like ATLAS.ti as well as in grounded theory research, which was used as a model for developing the program, codes address above all the contents of a text, so that the formal quality of a sequence is a second level of coding. Here you should define a way of how to double code material right from the beginning of a study using triangulation.

## Interfaces between QDA and statistics software

In studies using triangulation with qualitative and quantitative methods, the question arises of how to link the data and analyses referring to them at the level of the computer also. None of the QDA programs aims at or offers tools for statistical analyses inside the program. SPSS is not prepared for administration and analysis of textual data (at the level of text, i.e. without coding in numbers). Therefore, different programs are used for the standardized and non-standardized parts of a study. This leads to questions of interfaces: can both program types be linked, can data and analyses done with ATLAS.ti, for example, be transferred into SPSS? The more recent versions of the programs offer such an option in both directions, which means they allow including information coming from SPSS. Here again, we should think about how to avoid any requirements coming from the program influencing data and analyses. This discussion has been going on for a while for the QDA programs in some detail. Empirical studies, however, have demonstrated that the types of analysis have not been reduced to specific methods because of the use of computers (see Fielding and Lee, 1998). More concrete examples of how to import demographic data (from SPSS) into analyses with Nudist can be found in Bazeley (2003), and suggestions of how to use both types of data in an integrated way with the program WinMax/MaxQDA are given by Kuckartz (1995).

116

# Presentation of studies using triangulation

For the presentation of results and procedures in studies using triangulation, several general problems, which are known for presenting qualitative research in general, occur again more seriously. First, an understandable and straightforward presentation, that is, one that is appropriate to the potential reader in its length, is much more difficult than for quantitative studies, if we want to present not only results but also the ways in which we produced them (see Lüders, 2004b). Quantitative results can be more easily presented in the form of tables, numbers and distributions. At the same time, quantitative results are often processed at a much higher level of aggregation than in qualitative research. In surveys, you will rarely work with results at the level of the single case, whereas in qualitative research the case study is often the first step and a comparative analysis only the second step also when presenting the research.

The first necessity for presenting a study using triangulation seems to be to make the different methodological procedures in themselves understandable and also how the triangulation was applied concretely, and finally to give examples of how results have been linked. In the end, the presentation should make clear why triangulation was used and why it was appropriate and necessary (see Gibbs, 2007; Rapley, 2007).

# Position of triangulation in the research process

### Exploration

As the preceding chapters may have shown already, triangulation can be used for different purposes and in different steps in the research process in order to advance the quality of qualitative research. For example, we can find from time to time that focus groups are used for exploring the research issue. The results from the focus groups in such a case are only used for preparing the actual data collection in, for example, semi-structured interviews but not as a stand-alone part of the study or the overall results.

### Data collection

Furthermore, various methods of data collection can be combined. To remain in the example, semi-structured single interviews and focus groups are done that address different aspects of the issue. The data are then analyzed using the same method (for example, theoretical coding according to Glaser and Strauss, 1967). The different data are perhaps brought together in one set of data. Triangulation then remains limited to data collection.

## Data interpretation

In a similar way, we can triangulate different methods of data interpretation by using it for data collected with one method. An example is to use (open or axial) coding according to Strauss (1987) in combination with applying a hermeneutic method to selected excerpts from a narrative interview. Roller et al. (1995) point in a similar direction with their suggestion of a hermeneutic-classificatory content analysis. Here, the triangulation remains restricted to the step of analyzing the data. In a similar way, we can use it in both steps when we use different techniques for analyzing data collected using different methods.

## Generalization

Another purpose for using triangulation can be the generalization of results. Whereas, for quantitative research, generalization is mainly a numerical problem, which is to be solved by statistical means, this issue is more complicated for qualitative research. For a start, the issue of generalization comes up in a similar way: a limited number of cases selected according to certain criteria (sometimes only one case) have been studied. The results claim validity beyond the material (cases, etc.) included in the study. Cases, groups, and so on in the study represent something more general. The issue of generalization comes up in qualitative research often in a fundamentally different way, as a part of this research is aiming at developing grounded theories from empirical material. Then generalization addresses the question, on which other contexts the developed theory can be transferred or for which other contexts it is valid beyond the one it was discovered in. Therefore, an approach for assessing qualitative research (pursuing this aim) is to ask which considerations and steps were undertaken to define and perhaps to extend the area of validity of empirical results or theories developed from them.

A starting point for this assessment is to reflect on how the researchers analyzed their cases and how they proceeded from their cases to more general statements. The special problem of generalization for qualitative research is that its starting point is often an analysis that is referred to a context, one specific case in this context and the conditions, relations and processes in it. This reference to context (often) gives qualitative research its specific significance. In generalization, this reference to a context is given up for analyzing how far the results are valid independently and beyond specific contexts. In tapering this dilemma, Lincoln and Guba (1985) address this issue under the headline: 'The only generalization is: there is no generalization'. However, they outline criteria and ways for generalizing insights beyond one context, when they suggest criteria such as the transferability of results from one context to another and fittingness as the degree of comparability of different contexts.

Different ways and means are discussed of how to mark out the road from the case to the theory in such a way that at least a certain generalization can be reached. A first step is to clarify the question of what degree of generalization is intended with the single study at all and can be reached, so that appropriate claims for generalization can be derived. A second step is to carefully include different cases and contexts, in which the issues are analyzed empirically. Generalizability of results is often closely linked to realizing the sample. Theoretical sampling offers a strategy for designing the variation of conditions, under which a phenomenon is studied, as broadly as possible. The third starting point is the systematic comparison of the collected materials. Triangulation can contribute to generalization in this sense. Here, the aim of triangulation is to transfer the results obtained at one level (e.g. knowledge) to a different level (e.g. practices) by using a second method of data collection. Seen more generally, when combining different (e.g. qualitative and quantitative) methods, it should be sorted out which logic (numerical or theoretical) generalization in this study should follow and how far each approach to generalization can be transferred from one method to the other.

## Quality criteria for studies using triangulation

Although we consider triangulation here mainly in the context of how to use it for advancing the quality of qualitative research, we can also ask the other way round: what constitutes the quality of a study using triangulation, how can it be assessed? If we want to assess a study using triangulation or its planning, we can think of different aspects.

### Compatibility of criteria

First of all, we have to consider for studies combining qualitative and quantitative methods that the quality criteria in each area cannot simply be applied to the other. In a consistent triangulation of both approaches, we should avoid the assessment of the whole study being dominated by one of the approaches (and its criteria). We should try to take the particularity of both approaches into account also for using criteria or for quality assessment in general. As should have become evident in earlier chapters, there is a very limited consensus about quality and criteria inside qualitative research among different researchers and research perspectives. Accordingly, we should consider the perhaps different claims for quality in each approach when we combine several qualitative methods and also the appropriateness of the criteria in each case.

### Quality of studies using triangulation

For answering the question of quality of studies using triangulation, we should first consider if and how far the combination of different methods has taken into account the theoretical and methodological background of each method. Second, we should look at the relation in which the single methods were placed towards each other: have they been used on equal footing, or was one used only in an exploratory way and the other as the main method? Third, we should see if each method was used and treated by itself in a consistent way. Finally, it should become clear for any study using triangulation why the extra effort of using different methods was made and that they accessed different levels and aspects of the phenomenon under study.

## Conclusion

In summary, planning a study using triangulation comes with various problems. They are located between several aspects: a sufficiently consistent application of a combination of different methodological backgrounds, and a treatment of both approaches in the design and planning of the study with equal weight for both methods. The question is whether the efforts of triangulation are in a sound relation to the advantage for answering the research question or promoting the quality of the research and finally the available resources. If these aspects are sufficiently considered, triangulation is a worthwhile strategy for extending the knowledge potential compared to single methods studies. The profits can be seen in two respects: (1) It produces far more profound, detailed and comprehensive results. (2) Because of this, it is a strategy for advancing the quality of qualitative research by showing off the limits of single methods (or approaches) and by overcoming them.

Perhaps we can end this brief overview of the use of triangulation as a strategy for advancing the quality of qualitative research with two quotations, marking the tensional field in which triangulation is located:

> There is no magic in triangulation. (Patton, 1980, p. 330)

> Triangulation is expensive. Weak designs may result from its implementation. However, its use, when coupled with sophisticated rigor, will broaden, thicken, and deepen the interpretive base of any study. (Denzin, 1989, p. 247)

In the remainder of the book, we will address strategies of managing the quality of qualitative research with the focus of ethics and transparency of research.

### ▤ Key points

- Triangulation can be an approach for promoting the quality of qualitative research.
- It comes with some (extra) practical problems resulting from the different logics of methods (or approaches) that are combined.

- Triangulation is not necessary in every case, but if it is used the practical problems mentioned here need some attention and then it can be helpful.

## Further reading

In the following texts such practical problems in general and for using triangulation are unfolded in more detail:

Denzin, N.K. (1989) *The Research Act* (3rd edn). Englewood Cliffs, NJ: Prentice-Hall.

Flick, U. (2006a) *An Introduction to Qualitative Research* (3rd edn). London: Sage.

Flick, U. (2007) *Designing Qualitative Research* (Book 1 of *The SAGE Qualitative Research Kit*). London: Sage

Gibbs, G. (2007) *Analyzing Qualitative Data* (Book 6 of *The SAGE Qualitative Research Kit*). London: Sage.

# 9
# Quality, creativity and ethics: different ways to ask the question

**Chapter objectives**
After reading this chapter, you should understand

- the complex relation of quality and ethics in qualitative research;
- that quality can be a preveguisite for ethical soundness of research;
- that strong claims for rigor and quality can lead to ethical problems; and
- the ethical dilemmas and dimensions in qualitative research and quality promotion.

Ethics are becoming increasingly relevant in the context of research. Most research has to be approved by institutional review boards. As qualitative research is almost always research with human beings in one way or the other, it has to be subjected to examination by institutional reviews quite regularly. Approval by ethic commissions or institutional review boards is linked to assessing the quality of (planned) research in a specific way, or to assessing specific aspects of quality of research. Most professional organizations of researchers, such as the British Sociological Association, have formulated and published their codes of ethics (see Flick, 2006a, chap. 4 for an overview). These codes of ethics are another way to institutionalize a check of the quality of (planned) research in its ethical dimensions. These brief remarks already show that there is a specific relation between the ethics of research, which is the actual purpose of such an institutionalized assessment or regulations, and the quality of research in its different facets. This relation will be addressed in this chapter from different angles in a little more detail.

## Research as intervention

Any form of research is an intervention that disturbs, influences or even changes the context in which the study is done. Interviewees are confronted with sometimes disturbing questions, routines of daily life or professional work are disrupted, and in evaluation research, for example, its results often aim at changing professional or institutional routines. Such an intervention has a specific ethical dimension to it, which has been discussed for public health and clinical research (Green and Thorogood, 2004). Here, four principles of research ethics have been developed against the background of healthcare ethics:

- autonomy – respecting the rights of the individual;
- beneficence – doing good;
- non-maleficence – not doing harm;
- justice – particularly distributive justice or equity (2004, p. 53).

These ethical principles are basically oriented on respecting the interests of participants by not hurting them or by not taking a unilateral position in the field against (other) members' interests. At the same time, interventions should bring an advantage to the field under study, more or less directly. Research is justified if it produces insights that advance what is known or contributes to solving problems – by new knowledge or by concrete suggestions for practical implications. To be beneficent in such a way, research has to meet some more general expectations. It should have a relevant research question and a clear research design that allows this research question to be answered and it should be done in such a way that the results can be trusted or are reliable so that interventions based on them are justified. These brief remarks show the relevance of quality issues in (qualitative) research for ethical issues. The intervention of research in a field and the disturbances it brings with it are only justified if it is done for good, reliable and trustworthy research that is as likely as possible to produce credible results. Impositions by research and researchers to participants or fields are only justified if the research is well done in the planning, in applying the methods and in interpreting the data. This is the dimension of the ethical justification of research in the field.

## Relevance of research as prerequisite for ethical soundness

This ethical justification implies the relevance of research as one dimension. Relevance again is closely linked to creativity, which means producing something new, or so far unknown, by doing the research. This starts from the research question, which should address a new or unanswered question. It continues secondly with the selection of designs and methods able to answer this question in a way that produces knowledge, which allows progress in the area of research – for the participants in the study or people in a similar situation. Let us take an example from my own research. In a current study, we focus on health concepts and health experiences of homeless adolescents (see Flick and Röhnsch, 2006, 2007). The research is based on two methodological approaches. In episodic interviews, we ask for concepts and relevance of health, how far this is a topic for the participants, which problems and practices the participants experience in different areas and what their experience with the health system has been. We also do participant observation in areas where homeless adolescents hang out and meet peers in a similar situation to themselves. Homelessness is defined according to hanging out at such spots, having an unstable housing situation at least for some time, or repeatedly participating in panhandling in the streets.

From an ethical point of view, several points become relevant. This group of people is a highly vulnerable population. For many of them, a way back into a 'normal' life of school, job, housing, family, and so on is unlikely, but not impossible. Health is a topic they normally do not think about much (as with most people) and which has a low priority for them compared to other problems they have to solve (where to spend the night, where to get money, and the like). At the same time, their life is full of health risks or risks that may affect their health. These range from living outdoors (sometimes in extreme cold or heat) to sexual risks (protection against sex with strangers who might be HIV-positive or carrying sexually transmitted diseases) to violence, drugs, alcohol and bad eating habits. Asking them to be ready for observation or to participate in an interview makes them aware and maybe alert to things in their life they normally do not think about much. In particular, the interview confronts the participants with sometimes unpleasant issues like sexual practices, moral issues like prostitution, health issues like acute or chronic illness, or unpleasant experiences with doctors and the like. All in all, interviewing them includes a strong confrontation with their own situation and the negative sides to it. This is also the case with other vulnerable people, like chronically ill people, patients in general or families with problems. In all these cases, such a confrontation should be justified by doing 'good' research starting from the expectation of producing new and credible insights that have not been available before and which may contribute to improving the situation of the participants or of people in a similar situation.

In the case of our example, the relevance of research comes on the one hand from the fact there was no similar research so far – at least not in Germany, where our project is located – and that this target group was widely neglected in the public discussion and in the health system. On the other hand, the aim of the research is to produce suggestions for improving the health situation and services for this target group against the background of our research. These aspects may justify the intervention in this life world from an ethical point of view.

This example should illustrate the relation of relevance of research and ethical soundness based on issues of appropriateness and a benefit/costs relation for the target group of the research.

## Quality of research as prerequisite for ethical appropriateness

As in the example already mentioned, quality of research can be seen as a prerequisite for ethically appropriate research. If I do interviews on sensitive topics with vulnerable people, for example, several quality aspects become relevant for making the research ethically appropriate. From a technical point of view, I should be able to apply the interview correctly, so that I know how to formulate questions and when to probe, so that the interview really helps to address and reveal the relevant issues of the topic (and of the interviewee's situation). From an ethical point of view, I should be sensitive about where to probe (or not), how to mediate questions of a sensitive topic, and where to give the participants room for talking about aspects that are important for them at this moment (even if they are not immediately relevant according to the interview schedule). It is also important to build up a relationship with the interviewees that allows them to explore their situation and the issue of the interview from their point of view and to trust the interviewer.

At the same time it is important not to make a false promise – to be clear that the relation between the researcher and participants is a research relation and not therapy or friendship and has an end-point built in. To be able to conduct a good interview in this sense is a starting point for doing ethically appropriate research – although it is not the only one. Another point is, for example, a clear idea of why to interview this specific person or group – which can be understood as a quality issue in respect to sampling and design in general. Finally, the planning of research should also include which aspects can be left out – which areas of participants' personal situations it is not necessary to address for answering the research question, which details are not necessary to document in the data, and so on. This means that a quality of (qualitative) research is to know the limits of what is necessary and to confine the research to those limits. The quality of writing about the research includes from an ethical point of view respecting those details of the participants' private life that can be left out without undermining the message of the findings. In the end, the quality of generalizations (what can I infer from my results, to whom can I extend their meaning beyond those whom I interviewed, for example?) becomes an issue of high ethical relevance. The same applies to the formulation of practical implications from my results. Are generalizations and implications really based on empirical evidence and on legitimate interpretations of data? Is it ethically sound and appropriate to draw them?

These exemplary questions concerning the quality of qualitative research can basically be summarized in the statement: only research of high quality can be ethically appropriate. But if we look the other way around, the question arises whether high-quality research already means that the research is ethically sound.

## Ethical principles in qualitative research

As in any other form of research with human beings, some principles have become essential as ethical principles in qualitative research also. Most of them are more or less directly linked to what has been said before about the ethics of intervention (see above), but something more specific has to be said here. Today it is some kind of an ethical standard to work on the basis of informed consent with participants, which means informing them about the research and that they are part of a research project and asking them formally (a written and signed contract) or, where this is not possible, informally (an oral agreement) to join the project. This should include giving the necessary information and clarification about the aims and expectations of the research and the chance for the person to refuse participation. There are exceptions to this rule, if we do research in open spaces (participant observation in a train station, for example) with many pedestrians who cannot all be asked for their consent. More complicated are cases with people who are not yet or no longer able to sign an interview contract (young children, very old people, specific illness situations) or give a consensus. Then it has to be carefully reflected who else can give this consensus and if this is appropriate.

In many cases, ethical issues are formalized in codes of ethics or in the consent of a committee of ethics or an institutional review board (see Flick, 2006a, chap. 4 for a more extended discussion). Such a formalization does not solve the ethical problems in the direct contact with people or the field. For example, a major challenge mentioned before is how to act neutrally as a researcher, which means not to advantage some members in the field and disadvantage others or not to become party to a conflict between members in the field. Finally, the protection of anonymity for the participants is a crucial issue and much more difficult to maintain than in large-scale survey research. Qualitative research, with its orientation to case studies, life histories, transcripts and real-world sites and the importance of context information for research, is confronted with problems in data protection that are much more difficult to handle.

## Ethical dilemmas in qualitative research

As perhaps has become evident so far, research ethics in general is something difficult to formalize; codes of ethics and institutional review boards do not prevent the researcher from having to make ethical decisions and reflections in the field. This is even more the case in qualitative research, where problems of invading people's private life are even more relevant than in quantitative research. The tension and the dilemma in qualitative research – as in ethics in general – are localized between the formulating of general rules of ethics and the day-to-day practices in the field and how to take these rules into account in these practices.

## Ethical dimensions in quality and validity discussions

Seen from the angle of quality in research, any research that is only duplicating existing research or which does not have the quality to contribute new knowledge to the existing knowledge can be seen as unethical (see, e.g., Department of Health, 2001). In such a notion, there is already a source for conflict. For judging the quality of research, the members of the ethics committee should have the necessary knowledge to assess a research proposal at a methodological level. This often means that the members of the committees – or at least some of the members – should be researchers themselves.

Lincoln (2005) mentions another issue in this context. In the US in particular, several trends can be observed. One is to subject any research that includes human beings to institutional review boards. Whereas this may be absolutely necessary for research affecting the physical state of people and its accompanying risks, for example in experiments with new medications, this is also extended to research based on interviewing or observing people without any physical intervention. It has long been debated whether or not such research should be assessed by institutional review boards (IRBs) or not (see above), and if so, whether the existing review boards are ready to assess qualitative research as they do with experimental research. Lincoln discusses several developments. One is that, for example, oral history research in general is now excluded from such an examination by the IRBs, with various consequences. It has the advantage that oral history projects can be done without such an examination, which could be helpful for other areas of qualitative research also. However, the other consequence is that oral history is relieved from this obligation of examination with the, at least, implicit argumentation that it is not really scientific research (which would be to examine), not even social science, but scholarship. Such a development would be dangerous for qualitative research if it was extended to all sorts of interview-based and ethnographic research in general. In such a case, qualitative research would lose its status as a social science to be taken seriously as both research and science.

On the other hand, Lincoln reports about the tendency to subject all forms of teaching qualitative research, which includes making research experience with people outside the classroom for students, a subject of examination of IRBs – unlike statistics teaching, for example (2005, p. 169). Failure of such an examination by an IRB means that the course cannot be held and assignments cannot be given. Lincoln sees this trend embedded in a movement to reduce science and scientific results in many areas like education, social work, health and the like to what meets the criteria of evidence and evidence-based knowledge. This again excludes a lot of qualitative research approaches and results from the realm of science (according to these criteria).

These examples show how quality- and standards-oriented discussions can turn into a moral argument about good and bad research – in general, not referring to the single project and its quality. They also show how a discussion and a trend, which were originally based on ethical considerations in one area (and which were more than necessary in this area) – medicine and public health – are generalized and functionalized when they are extended to the area of qualitative research. They are functionalized for disqualifying qualitative research against a specific understanding of science and also its very specific standards.

Guba and Lincoln (2005) discuss the current state of the debate about paradigms in qualitative research and the discussion about validity in these and qualitative research in general. What they show, basically in referring to discussions they inaugurated earlier with their suggestions for alternative criteria (Lincoln and Guba, 1985; Guba and Lincoln, 1989), is how the validity issue has moved in these discussion from a technical approach to the term and the problem to a much more moral and ethical discourse. For example, when they suggested authenticity and fairness as criteria for judging the quality of qualitative research, this is no longer a technical examination coming with a cut-off point or benchmark but a moral-ethical examination of how far researchers did justice to their participants in what they did. With reference to Lather's (1993) suggestion 'to bring ethics and epistemology together', Guba and Lincoln (2005, p. 209) consequently talk of 'validity as an ethical relationship'. In these suggestions and the consequences the authors draw from them, we have a close link between ethics and quality issues in a formerly methodological debate.

And there is another version of this relation between ethics and quality. In the beginning we spoke of quality in research as a prerequisite of ethical sound research. The more quality is based on methodological rigor, the more we are confronted with the danger that quality claims come with (negative) consequences for ethical concerns. To make patients give a narrative covering their whole life history in order to meet the methodological or quality requirements of a narrative method can be ethically problematic if this is stressful for already vulnerable persons and if this need is not really grounded in the research question. To subject such patients to the application of several methods – for meeting the standards of triangulation in order to increase the quality of the research – can be ethically problematic if it means extra stress for the persons and is not absolutely necessary. These examples may show that the relation between quality and ethics can become inverted at some points or under certain circumstances.

## Key points

- Quality issues and ethical concerns about qualitative research are closely linked in different respects.
- Qualitative (and other) research and the intervention in people's lives and in fields linked to it are only legitimate if it is creative, that is, it brings new insights into or solutions of problems.
- Quality of research is a precondition of ethically sound research.
- Qualitative research has difficulties in passing examinations by institutional review boards.
- Nevertheless it should avoid a status where it is no longer seen as relevant for such an examination.
- The discussions about quality in qualitative research have developed from a more technical-methodological problem to an issue of ethics in itself.
- Rigor in qualitative research can be a contribution to its quality, but can also come into conflict with research ethics in some cases.

### Further reading

In these texts, the parts of the relation between creativity as a legitimation of research and ethics and quality are discussed from different angles in more detail:

Flick, U. (2006a) *An Introduction to Qualitative Research* (3rd edn). London: Sage, chap. 4.

Guba, E.G. and Lincoln, Y.S. (2005) 'Paradigmatic controversies, contradictions, and emerging confluences', in N. Denzin and Y.S. Lincoln (eds), *Handbook of Qualitative Research* (3rd edn). Thousand Oaks, CA: Sage, pp. 191–215.

Lincoln, Y.S. (2005) 'Institutional review boards and methodological conservatism', in N. Denzin and Y.S. Lincoln (eds), *Handbook of Qualitative Research* (3rd edn). Thousand Oaks, CA: Sage, pp. 165–81.

# 10
# Managing quality in qualitative research: a focus on process and transparency

**Chapter objectives**
After reading this chapter, you should see

- the different ways of how to deal with the issue of quality from a research process approach;
- the importance of reflecting, on which methods or approaches to use;
- the relevance of defining claims of quality during the process of research by involving all members of the research team; and
- that the quality issue in qualitative research is to a large extent a problem of making research transparent.

In the preceding chapters of this book, I have addressed the issue of quality from different angles: by defining and applying criteria, by using strategies of managing or increasing diversity in the research process, and with reference to ethical issues. Common to these approaches to quality is that they pick up a certain point in the research process – like using methods for analyzing data or in assessing the quality of the relations to the field under study – for answering the questions of quality. In what follows, I will take a perspective that is more oriented to the research process as a whole. It starts from the 'why' of using specific methods, then it will continue with the 'how' of agreeing about quality issues before ending with 'how far' we can make such a process transparent to the consumers of our research.

## Indication of methods and designs

Why do we use a specific method of qualitative research for studying a specific issue? Is it always the appropriateness of methods to issues that drives us in our decision for one method and against other ones? Is this relation of appropriateness so clearly defined that it makes decisions easy, clear and obvious? Or do many of our colleagues not simply do what they always did: do they not just simply continue with methods they used before when they start a new project? Perhaps a look at the life record of qualitative researchers and the methods they used over the years will show a limited variation in the application of methods in many cases. These questions bring us to a way of how to make the decision for a specific method and/or a specific research design more explicit. In methodology discussions mainly in textbooks, research methods are mostly focused on as side-by-side issues for describing their features, advantages and problems. A comparative perspective, which would give the reader a rationale for deciding when to use this method or design and when not to use it, is seldom taken.

Here, we face a similar problem as therapists or physicians, who have to decide which of the methods or interventions they have learned and are at hand they should use in a specific case of intervention. In these contexts, this problem is discussed as the 'indication' of treatments. In medicine or psychotherapy, practitioners check the appropriateness of a certain treatment for specific problems and groups of people. The result of this check is whether or not a specific treatment is indicated (i.e. appropriate) for a specific problem in a concrete case. If we transfer this to qualitative research, the relevant questions are, when are which qualitative methods appropriate – to which issue? to which research question? to which group of people (population) or fields to be studied? and so on. When are quantitative methods or a combination of both indicated? How to make this decision and the indication transparent to readers and other consumers of the research? (see Table 10.1).

TABLE 10.1   Indication of qualitative research methods

| Psychotherapy and medicine | | | Qualitative research | | |
|---|---|---|---|---|---|
| Which disease, symptoms, diagnosis, population | **indicate** | Which treatment or therapy ? | Which issue, population, research question, knowledge of issue and population | **indicate** | Which method or methods? |

1   When is which method appropriate and indicated?
2   How to make a rational decision for or against certain methods?
3   How to make this decision and the indication transparent to readers and other consumers of the research?

Indication in qualitative research means basically three things, if we look at it from the angle of quality in the research process: (1) To select the appropriate method by taking into account to whom or what it shall be applied. (2) To document this selection process and the decisions taken in it and why they were taken. (3) And finally, to make this process transparent to the reader or consumer of the research. The core of this is how to select a qualitative research method. Table 10.2 provides a number of orienting questions, most of them developed elsewhere (Flick, 2006a, p. 386), where they are unfolded in more detail.

TABLE 10.2   Guiding questions for selecting a qualitative research method

| | |
|---|---|
| 1 | What do I know about the issue of my study or how detailed is my knowledge already? |
| 2 | How developed is the theoretical or empirical knowledge in the literature about the issue? |
| 3 | Is my interest in more generally exploring the field and the issue of my study? |
| 4 | What is the theoretical background of my study and which methods fit this background? |
| 5 | What do I want to get close to in my study: personal experiences of (a group) of certain people or social processes in the making? Or am I more interested in reconstructing the underlying structures of my issue? |
| 6 | Do I start with a very focused research question right away or do I start from a rather unfocused approach in order to develop the more focused questions underway in the process of my project? |
| 7 | Which aggregate do I want to study: personal experiences, interactions or situations or bigger entities like organizations or discourse? |
| 8 | Is it more the single case (e.g. of a personal illness experience or of a certain institution) I am interested in or the comparison of various cases? |
| 9 | Which resources (time, money, (wo)/manpower, skills, etc) are available for my study? |
| 10 | What are the characteristics of the field I want to study and of the people in it? What can you request of them and what not? |
| 11 | What is the claim of generalization of my study? |
| 12 | What are the ethical issues to take into account that are affected by selecting a specific method? |

Arguments that a specific method should be used in qualitative research as the right and only method are no longer adequate given the proliferation of the area. However, we should plan our research methodologically and base it on principles and reflection. Sticking to fixed and well-defined paradigms runs the risk of obstructing the way to the issue under study rather than opening new and appropriate ways to it. Decisions for theory and method in qualitative research should be taken and reflected in a knowledge-based way. Table 10.3 presents some rules of thumb for making decisions along the research process and some key questions to reflect what has been decided and applied in the ongoing research process.

To think about the question of indication of qualitative research methods and approaches is the first step to basing the answers to the question of the quality of qualitative research on the research process. It is the first step in ensuring and enhancing the quality of qualitative research, which should be followed by strategies to enhance the quality of quality research such as those discussed in the earlier chapters. It should also be the entrance to a process of defining, clarifying and making explicit what is understood as quality – not in general at the level of the textbook this time, but for the concrete ongoing research project and for those who are involved in it as researchers.

TABLE 10.3    Rules of thumb and key questions for reflecting research steps and methods

---

1    Decide and reflect carefully whether qualitative or quantitative research.
     Why qualitative research?
     Which reasons do you have for the one or the other?
     What are your expectations for the (qualitative) research that you plan?

2    Reflect on the theoretical background of your knowledge interest.
     What is the impact of your setting on the research?
     How open and how closed is your access to what you want to study?

3    Plan your study carefully, but allow for reconsidering the steps and modifying according to the state of the study.
     What are the resources available for the study?
     How realistic are the aims of your research in relation to the available resources?
     What are necessary and appropriate shortcuts?

4    Plan your sampling carefully!
     What are your cases?
     What do they stand for?

5    Think about whom in the field you should contact and inform about your research. Reflect about the relation to establish to field subjects.
     What can you learn about your research field and issues from the way you get into the field or are rejected?

6    Think about why you chose the special method of collecting data.
     Was it a decision for a favourite method (the one you or your colleagues have always used) for habitual reasons?
     What could or would alternative methods provide?
     What are the impacts of the methods you use on your data and your knowledge?

---

*(Continued)*  **133**

**TABLE 10.3** *(Continued)*

7  Plan carefully how to document your data and research experiences.
   How exactly should you write your notes?
   What do you need as information to document systematically?
   What are the influences of the documentation on your research and on your field subjects?
   What are the impacts of the documentation on your methods of collection and analysis?

8  Think about the aims of your data analysis.
   Was it a decision for a favourite method (the one you or your colleagues have always used) for habitual reasons?
   What could or would alternative methods provide?
   What are the impacts of the methods you use on your data and your knowledge?

9  Think about the way you want to present what you have experienced in the field and found in your research.
   What are the target audiences of your writing?
   What is it mainly you want to convince them about your research?
   What is the impact of the format of your writing on your research and its findings?

10 Plan how to establish the quality of your research.
   What are the quality criteria your research should meet?
   How should these criteria be realized?
   What is their impact on your research and your field subjects or relationships?

11 Think carefully about whether or not you want to use computers and software in the research.
   Which computers or software do you want to use?
   What are your expectations and aims in using them?
   Why do you use them?
   What is their impact on your research and your field subjects or relationships?

(From Flick (2006a) pp. 388–9).

# Quality management in qualitative research

In Chapter 2, it was mentioned that standards of qualitative research should be reconstructed from the research practice (see Bohnsack, 2005). Going one step further, the concept of quality management in qualitative research is more anchored in the research practice itself. Quality management has been discussed for some time in the context of industrial production or services or in the health system. This approach can be transferred to qualitative research for advancing the discussion about quality in qualitative research. First links exist in the concept of auditing, which is discussed in both areas. Lincoln and Guba (1985) suggest a process of auditing for assessing the reliability of qualitative data, which is oriented on accounting in financial contexts. An auditing trail includes:

- the raw data, their collection and recording;
- data reduction and results of syntheses by summarizing, theoretical notes, memos, etc., summaries, short descriptions of cases, etc.;
- reconstruction of data and results of syntheses according to the structure of developed and used categories (themes, definitions, relationships), findings (interpretations and inferences) and the reports produced with their integration of concepts and links to the existing literature;
- process notes, i.e. methodological notes and decisions concerning the production of trustworthiness and credibility of findings;
- materials concerning intentions and dispositions like the concepts of research, personal notes and expectations of the participants;
- information about the development of the instruments including the pilot version and preliminary plans (see Lincoln and Guba, 1985, pp. 320–7, 382–4).

Here, a process perspective is already taken, which includes all relevant steps of the research process that have led to the data and their interpretation. In the context of quality management, 'an audit is understood as a systematic, independent examination of an activity and its results, by which the existence and appropriate application of specified demands are evaluated and documented' (Kamiske and Brauer, 1995, p. 5). In particular, the 'procedural audit' is interesting for qualitative research. It should guarantee that 'the pre-defined demands are fulfilled and are useful for the respective application. … Priority is always given to an enduring remedy of causes of mistakes, not only a simple detection of mistakes' (Kamiske and Brauer, 1995, p. 8). Such specifications of quality are not conducted abstractly, for example, for certain methods per se, but with regards to the client orientation (pp. 95–6) and the co-workers' orientation (pp. 110–11).

On the first point, the question that results is who the clients of qualitative research actually are. Quality management distinguishes internal and external clients. Whereas the latter are the consumers of the product, the former are those who are involved in its production in a broader sense (e.g. employees in other departments). For qualitative research, this distinction may be translated as follows. External clients are those outside the project for whom its results are produced (overseers, reviewers, etc., as external clients). Internal clients then are those for and with whom one attempts to obtain the result (interviewees, institutions under study, etc.). Concepts like 'member checks' or communicative validation (see Chapter 2) explicitly take this orientation into account. Designing the research process and proceeding in a way that gives enough room to those who are studied, realizes this orientation implicitly. For an evaluation, both aspects may be analyzed explicitly: how far did the study proceed in a way that it answered its research question (orientation on external clients) and did it give enough room to the perspectives of those who were involved as interviewees, for example (orientation on internal clients)? The co-worker orientation wants to take into account that 'quality arises from applying suitable techniques but on the basis of a corresponding mentality' (Kamiske and Brauer, 1995, p. 110). Transferred to qualitative research, this underlines that not only the application of methods essentially determines its quality, but also the attitude with which the research is conducted. Another point of departure here is the 'to give responsibility [for quality] to the co-workers by introducing self-assessments instead of outside control' (Kamiske and Brauer, 1995, p. 111). Quality in the qualitative research process can be realized, as elsewhere, if it is produced and assessed together with the researchers involved. First, they define together what should be and what is understood as quality in this context. Quality management then includes 'activities ... defining the quality policy, the goals and the responsibilities and realizing these by means of quality planning, quality steering, quality assessment/quality management and quality improvement' (ISO 9004, quoted in Kamiske and Brauer, 1995, p. 149).

Quality in the qualitative research process can only be realized when it is produced and assessed with all researchers involved in the project in a shared activity. First, they should define what they understand as quality in the context of the current project. For this, we can use the following guideline of quality management in qualitative research:

- Develop a definition of which goals should be reached in the project and of which standards should be maintained. This definition should be as clear as possible. All researchers in the project should be integrated in developing this definition.
- Define how to realize these goals and standards, and more generally the quality to be obtained. Therefore, develop a consensus about how to apply the selected methods. For example, joint interview training and its analysis can become preconditions for quality in the research process.
- Develop a clear definition of the responsibilities for obtaining quality in the research process for each researcher.
- Establish as much transparency of the judgement and the assessment of quality in the process as possible.
- Therefore establish research diaries and protocols of the research process and the decisions taken in it.

In contrast to other ways of assessing the quality of qualitative research, in quality management all members of the research team will discuss and define what they understand as quality in their project, which quality goals follow from this definition and how to reach these goals in detail. In this concept, the idea is given up that research quality should be defined generally, in an abstract way and from the outside. This idea is given up in favour of a joint clarification of the concept of quality and of how to make it work (for more details, see also Flick, 2006a, chap. 29).

# Quality of qualitative research as a result of a decision process

As the preceding chapters should have made clear, quality in qualitative research is more than just defining criteria or standards and – simply – meeting or fulfilling them. According to what has been said so far, quality is the result of a series of decisions starting from the formulation of a research question, continuing with finding and using the appropriate methods for working on answering this question. It has a lot to do with – or can be advanced a lot by using – strategies for managing diversity and for extending the knowledge potential in the project and in the data. Quality is linked with ethical issues in several ways and is closely connected with the transparency produced in the research and for the reader or consumers of the result. For a long time, much of qualitative research was driven by an idea about the one and only way to do qualitative research. This idea was for a long time dominant in qualitative research and fed by the attitude of criticism against other forms of research. If we abandon such an idea of qualitative research, a project consists of a series of decisions about how to proceed, about which alternatives to reject, and so on. These decisions should be driven by the overall guideline of (qualitative) research: that methods and procedures should be appropriate to what and to who is studied and should be useful for answering the research question in a way that is methodologically and ethically sound. Quality then is something that should be made explicit in how it is defined, should be managed in the steps of such a decision process and produced step by step. If we want to take quality in qualitative research out of the realm of the vague and mysterious, of the abstract and fundamental, a necessary part of it is to communicate what is understood as quality and how it was produced in the process.

# Transparency, documentation and writing

In this context, transparency becomes relevant in several ways for enhancing the quality of qualitative research. Transparency means in general to make the research process, in its steps and in the decisions that influenced how data and results were produced, understandable to readers in the broadest sense. Transparency means to document how the research question was developed in the first step and how it perhaps was changed in the course of the project. It should also be documented why which persons, groups, cases, situations, and so on, were selected as empirical material – what the rationale of the sampling was and how the researchers made it work. Following what was said before, the documentation and the report about the project and the research should provide insights into why specific methods were selected, perhaps which alternatives were discussed and why they were rejected – in short, how the question of indication was handled and answered. Information about the claims for quality in the project, how they were set up, who was involved in defining them and finally how they were realized are another issue of documentation – in short, how the quality management in the project was planned and realized.

Following what was said in Chapter 3, it seems necessary to address the question of diversity in the documentation and to make transparent how deviant cases and perspectives of third parties like members or audiences were treated and integrated in the progress of the research. Seen in this way, transparency starts from a detailed documentation of the research process, its steps and the decisions taken in it. This documentation should find its way into the report about the research and about how results were produced. In the best examples it should not only make transparent what was done and why, but also allow the reader to obtain an idea of how different the results would have been if the researchers had taken a different decision at some specific point. Then it comes close to the function that Lüders sees for the report about the research:

> The research report with its presentation of and reflection on the methodological proceedings, with all its narratives about access to and the activities in the field, with its documentation of various materials, with its transcribed observations and conversations, interpretations and theoretical inferences is the only basis for answering the question of the quality of the investigation. (Lüders, 1995, p. 325)

Reichertz (1992) goes one step beyond a text-centred treatment of credibility. He makes it clear that this form of persuasion concerning credibility is produced not only in the text but also in the interaction of author, text and reader:

> The decisive point, however, is the attitude which is expressed in the text, with which the ethnographer turns toward his own interpretations and those of his colleagues in order to relate them to each other according to the needs of the individual case. It is not the way of accounting claimed for in the writing which is relevant for the reader, but the attitude of accounting which is shown in the text, which of course always has to use semiotic means, and these are means which are sensitive to cheating. (1992, p. 346)

Thus, to do qualitative research in a way that meets high standards and expectation is one thing. To address the issue of quality in the research process – by meeting standards, by using strategies, and so on, – is a second thing. But this will only become visible as quality in qualitative research, if the researchers manage to transfer their aims and claims, their strategies and standards and how they worked with them to the readers of their research. In this way, writing about research is the third and maybe most important part of qualitative research if we want to assess the goodness of research or if we want to allow readers to assess it. Writing then becomes not only a technical problem, but also an issue of reflexivity – but in a different sense from what has been discussed so vehemently as the crisis of representation (Denzin and Lincoln, 2000) in the last few years. Writing about research and the procedures used in it (see Flick, 2006a, chap 30) becomes an important instrument for conveying what was done in the project, how it was done and how well it was done.

### ▰▰▰ Key points

- Quality in qualitative research is produced (or fails) through the whole process of research.
- Clarifying the issue of indication of methods and designs is a crucial step in establishing quality in the research.
- The advantage of a quality management approach to qualitative research is that it starts from developing a shared understanding of quality and quality aims for the current project in which all researchers should be involved.
- It also understands quality as something to be developed, maintained and produced throughout the whole project.
- Transparency is based on documentation and the crucial step in transferring to the readers or consumers what was done for promoting quality and how it was done and the results to which it led.
- Writing about the research is a precondition for making research processes and procedures transparent to readers or consumers.

### Further reading

In these texts, the building blocks of writing, quality management, indication and process quality are unfolded in more detail:

Becker, H.S. (1986) *Writing for Social Scientists.* Chicago: University of Chicago Press.

Flick, U. (2006a) *An Introduction to Qualitative Research* (3rd edn). London: Sage, part 7.

Lincoln, Y.S. and Guba, E.G. (1985) *Naturalistic Inquiry.* London: Sage.

# ▌▌▌ Glossary

**Analytic induction** Strategy for using negative/deviant cases to assess and elaborate findings, models or theories developed.

**ATLAS.ti** Software for supporting the qualitative analysis of text, images and other data in qualitative research.

**Auditing** Strategy for assessing a process (in accounting or in research) in all its steps and components.

**Benchmark** Cut-off point for distinguishing good/bad or successful/unsuccessful research.

**Between-methods triangulation** Combination of two independent methods in studying one issue.

**Bias** Disturbing influence on research and results.

**Communicative validation** Assessment of results (or of data) by asking the participants for their consensus.

**Comprehensive triangulation** Combination of the different forms of triangulation (investigator, theory, methods and data) in one mode.

**Constant comparative method** Part of grounded theory methodology focusing on comparing all elements in the data with each other.

**Credibility** Criterion for evaluating qualitative research based on prolonged engagement in the field.

**Criteria** Instruments for assessing the quality of research, ideally coming with a cut-off point (benchmark), to distinguish good from bad research.

**Data triangulation** Combination of different forms of data.

**Deviant case** Case not fitting in or supporting a model or other forms of findings.

**Episodic interview** Interview combining question/answer sequences with narratives (of episodes).

**Evaluation** Use of research methods for estimating and deciding about the success of an intervention.

**Evidence-based practices** Interventions (in medicine, social work, nursing, etc.) that are based on results of research.

**External validity** How far do the results of a study apply to situations outside the actual research situation?

**Falsification** Testing theories by trying to show that they are not correct.

**Generalization** Transfer of research results to situations and populations that were not part of the research situation.

**Hybrid methodologies** Methodologies that include elements from more than one method or approach (e.g. in ethnography).

**Hypothesis** In standardized research, assumptions to be tested in research. In qualitative research, hypotheses are used in a more meta-phorical sense (e.g. as working hypothesis) without being formulated before the research and being tested.

**Indication** Decision about when exactly (under which conditions) a specific method (or combination of methods) should be used.

**Informed consent** Participants in a study are informed that they are studied and given the chance to say no to the research.

**Internal validity** Degree of control of the research situation through standardization.

**Investigator triangulation** Combination of more than one researcher either in collaboration or independently for promoting the quality of the research.

**Likert scale** Questions in a questionnaire with five (sometimes seven) standardized alternatives for answering, which can be ticked by the respondent.

**Managing quality** Means that quality in the qualitative research process has not only to be assessed but has to be produced throughout the research process by using criteria or strategies.

**MAXQDA** Software for analyzing qualitative data; earlier versions were called WinMax.

**Member checks** Assessment of results (or of data) by asking the participants for their consensus.

**Mixed methodologies** An approach of combining qualitative and quantitative methods at a rather pragmatic level.

**Narrative-episodic knowledge** Knowledge based on memories of situations and their concrete circumstances.

**Negative case** Case (or more generally, empirical material) not fitting in or supporting a model or other forms of findings.

**Non-standardized research** Different term for qualitative research stressing that the low(er) degree of standardization in the research situation is the distinctive feature from quantitative research.

**Nudist** Software for analyzing qualitative data; recent versions are called EnVivo.

**Objectivity** The degree to which a research situation (the application of methods and their outcome) is independent from the single researcher.

**Proposal** Research plan developed for applying for funding or in a PhD or master's program.

**QDA software** Qualitative data analysis software specially developed for supporting the analysis of texts like interviews and their coding, administration, etc. Examples are ATLAS.ti, MaxQDA or Nudist.

**Quality management** Approach for promoting the quality of a process with a stress on a common development and clarification of the standards to be met in the process involving all members of the team.

**Quality of life** A concept for analyzing the situation of living in the context of an illness or a treatment, mostly measured using standardized instruments like the SF-36.

**Relevance of research** How far do the research and its results contribute to developing new knowledge or new solutions to specific problems?

**Reliability** One of the standard criteria in standardized/quantitative research, measured for example by repeating a test and assessing whether the results are the same in both cases.

**Research design** A systematic plan for a research project, including who to integrate in the research (sampling), who or what to compare for which dimensions, etc.

**Sampling** The selection of cases, persons, materals, etc. to study from a bigger population or variety.

**Semantic-conceptual knowledge** Knowledge organized around concepts, their meaning and relations among each other.

**Semi-standardized interview** Interviews with a set of questions that can be asked in a different sequence and not in a strict standardized formulation (also called open interview).

**Sensitive topics** Issues in an interview, for example, that are not too easy to talk about (because they are embarrassing or stressful, e.g. because related to illness).

**SF-36** A standard questionnaire for analyzing the quality of life in the context of a health problem or treatment.

**Shortcut strategies** Pragmatic ways of using specific methods in situations of applied research, where it may be difficult to use these methods in their full versions (for example in the context of qualitative evaluation).

**Social representation** A concept for describing the knowledge of social groups about scientific findings or other issues.

**Standardization** The degree of controlling a research situation by defining and delimiting as many features of it as necessary or possible.

**Strategies (of managing quality)** Instead of using criteria for assessing research quality, strategies for improving this quality are employed.

**Subjective theory** Laypeople's knowledge about certain issues can be organized similarly to scientific theories (e.g. subjective theories of health or illness).

**Systematic triangulation of perspectives** The combination of different methods including their (differing) theoretical backgrounds in the study of one issue.

**Theoretical sampling** The sampling procedure in grounded theory research, where cases, groups or materials are sampled according to their relevance for the theory that is developed and against the background of what is already the state of knowledge after collecting and analyzing a certain number of cases.

**Theory triangulation** The combination of different theoretical perspectives in the study of one issue.

**Transparency** The degree of how far a reader of a research study is enabled to understand how the research went on in concrete terms.

**Triangulation** The combination of different methods, theories, data and/or researchers in the study of one issue.

**Triathlon** An extreme kind of sport combining running a marathon, swimming and cycling very long distances.

**Validity** One of the standard criteria in standardized/quantitative research, analyzed for example by looking for confounding influences (internal validity) or for the transferability to situations beyond the current research situation (external validity).

**Vulnerable population** People in a specific situation (social discrimination, risks, illness) that makes a specific sensitiveness necessary when studying them.

**Within-methods triangulation** The combination of two methodological approaches (e.g. question/answer and narratives) in one method.

# III References

Altheide, D.L. and Johnson, J.M. (1998) 'Criteria for assessing interpretive validity in qualitative research', in N. Denzin and Y.S. Lincoln (eds), *Collecting and Interpreting Qualitative Materials*. London: Sage, pp. 293–312.

Amann, K. and Hirschauer, S. (1997) 'Die Befremdung der eigenen Kultur. Ein Programm', in S. Hirschauer and K. Amann (eds), *Die Befremdung der eigenen Kultur. Zur ethnographischen Herausforderung soziologischer Empirie*. Frankfurt a. M.: Suhrkamp, pp. 7–52.

Angell, R.C. and Turner, R.H. (1954) 'Comment and reply on discussions of the analytic induction method', *American Sociological Review,* 19: 476–8.

Angrosino, M. (2007) *Doing Ethnographic and Observational Research* (Book 3 of *The SAGE Qualitative Research Kit*). London: Sage.

Atkinson, P., Coffey, A., Delamont, S., Lofland, J. and Lofland L. (eds) (2001) *Handbook of Ethnography*. London: Sage.

Banks, M. (2007) *Using Visual Data in Qualitative Research* (Book 5 of *The SAGE Qualitative Research Kit*). London: Sage.

Barbour, R. (2001) 'Checklists for improving rigour in qualitative research: a case of the tail wagging the dog?', *British Medical Journal,* 322: 1115–17.

Barbour, R. (2007) *Doing Focus Groups* (Book 4 of *The SAGE Qualitative Research Kit*). London: Sage.

Barton, A.H. and Lazarsfeld, P.F. (1955) 'Some functions of qualitative analysis in social research', *Frankfurter Beiträge zur Soziologie* I. Frankfurt a. M.: Europäische Verlagsanstalt, pp. 321–61.

Bateson, G. and Mead, M. (1942) *Balinese Character: A Photographic Analysis*, Vol. 2. New York: New York Academy of Sciences.

Bazeley, P. (2003) 'Computerized data analysis for mixed methods research', in A. Tashakkori and C. Teddlie (eds), *Handbook of Mixed Methods in Social and Behavioral Research*. Thousand Oaks, CA: Sage, 385–422.

Becker, H. and Geer, B.S. (1960) 'Participant observation: analysis of qualitative data', in R.N. Adams and J.J. Preiss (eds), *Human Organization Research*. Homewood, IL: Dorsey Press, pp. 267–89.

Becker, H.S. (1986) *Writing for Social Scientists*. Chicago: Chicago University Press.

Bergmann, J.R. (1985) 'Flüchtigkeit und methodische Fixierung sozialer Wirklichkeit. Aufzeichnungen als Daten der interpretativen Soziologie', in W. Bonss and H. Hartmann (eds), *Entzauberte Wissenschaft – Zur Realität und Geltung soziologischer Forschung*. Göttingen: Schwartz, pp. 299–320.

Blaikie, N.W. (1991) 'A critique of the use of triangulation in social research', *Quality and Quantity,* 25: 115–36.

Bloor, M. (1978) 'On the analysis of observational data: a discussion of the worth and uses of inductive techniques and respondent validation', *Sociology,* 12: 545–52.

# References

Bloor, M. (1997) 'Techniques of validation in qualitative research: a critical commentary', in G. Miller and R. Dingwall (eds), *Context and Method in Qualitative Research*. London: Sage, pp. 37–50.

Bohnsack, R. (2004) 'Group discussions and focus groups', in U. Flick, E. von Kardorff and I. Steinke (eds), *A Companion to Qualitative Research*. London: Sage, pp. 214–20.

Bohnsack, R. (2005) 'Standards nicht-standardisierter Forschung in den Erziehungs- und Sozialwissenschaften', *Zeitschrift für Erziehungswissenschaft*, 8(4): 63–81.

Brewer, J. and Hunter, A. (1989) *Multimethod Research: A Synthesis of Styles*. Newbury Park, CA: Sage.

Bruner, J. (1990) *Acts of Meaning*. Cambridge, MA: Harvard University Press.

Bruner, J. (2002) *Making Stories: Law, Literature, Life*. Cambridge, MA: Harvard University Press.

Bryman, A. (1992) 'Quantitative and qualitative research: further reflections on their integration', in J. Brannen (ed.), *Mixing Methods: Quantitative and Qualitative Research*. Aldershot: Avebury, pp. 57–80.

Bryman, A. (2004) *Social Research Methods* (2nd edn). Oxford: Oxford University Press.

Bühler-Niederberger, D. (1985) 'Analytische Induktionals Verfahren qualitativer Methodologie', *Zeitschrift für Soziologie*, 14: 475–85.

Campbell, D. and Fiske, D. (1959) 'Convergent and discriminant validation by the multi-trait-multimethod-matrix', *Psychological Bulletin*, 56: 81–105.

Cassell, C., Buehring, A., Symon, G., Johnson, P. and Bishop, V. (2005) *Qualitative Management Research: A Thematic Analysis of Interviews with Stakeholders in the Field*. Manchester: University of Manchester.

Cassell, C. and Symon, G. (eds) (2004) *Essential Guide to Qualitative Methods in Organizational Research*. London: Sage.

Charmaz, K. (2006) *Constructing Grounded Theory: A Practical Guide Through Qualitative Analysis*. Thousand Oaks, CA: Sage.

Clark, D. (1951) *Plane and Geodetic Surveying for Engineers*, Vol. 2. London: Constable.

Cressey, D.R. (1950) 'Criminal violation of final trust', dissertation, Indiana University.

Creswell, J.W. (2003) *Research Design: Qualitative, Quantitative, and Mixed Methods Approaches*. Thousand Oaks, CA: Sage.

Creswell, J.W., Plano Clark, V.L., Gutman, M.L. and Hanson, W.E. (2003) 'Advanced mixed methods research design', in A. Tashakkori and C. Teddlie (eds), *Handbook of Mixed Methods in Social and Behavioral Research*. Thousand Oaks, CA: Sage, pp. 209–40.

Dausien, B. and Kelle, H. (2003) 'Zur Verbindung von ethnographischen und biographischen Forschungsperspektiven', in J. Allmendinger (ed.), *Entstaatlichung und soziale Sicherheit*, CD-Supplement. Opladen: Leske & Budrich.

Deegan, M.J. (2001) 'The Chicago School of ethnography', in P. Atkinson, A. Coffey, S. Delamont, J. Lofland and L. Lofland (eds), *Handbook of Ethnography*. London: Sage, pp. 11–25.

Denzin, N.K. (1970) *The Research Act*. Chicago: Aldine.

Denzin, N.K. (1989) *The Research Act* (3rd edn). Englewood Cliffs, NJ: Prentice-Hall.

Denzin, N.K. (2004) 'Symbolic interactionism', in U. Flick, E. von Kardorff and I. Steinke (eds), *A Companion to Qualitative Research*. London: Sage, pp. 81–7.

Denzin, N. and Lincoln, Y.S. (eds) (1994) *Handbook of Qualitative Research*. London: Sage.

Denzin, N. and Lincoln, Y.S. (eds) (2000) *Handbook of Qualitative Research* (2nd edn). London: Sage.

Denzin, N. and Lincoln, Y.S. (eds) (2005) *Handbook of Qualitative Research* (3rd edn). London: Sage.

# References

Department of Health (2001) *Research Governance Framework for Health and Social Care*. London: Department of Health.

Douglas, J.D. (1976) *Investigative Social Research*. Beverly Hills, CA: Sage.

Elliot R., Fischer, C.T. and Rennie, D.L. (1999) 'Evolving guidelines for publication of qualitative research studies in psychology and related fields', *British Journal of Clinical Psychology*, 38: 215–29.

Fielding, N.G. and Fielding, J.L. (1986) *Linking Data*. Beverly Hills, CA: Sage.

Fielding, N.G. and Lee, R.M. (1998) *Computer Analysis and Qualitative Research*. London: Sage.

Fleck, C. (2004) 'Marie Jahoda' in U. Flick, E. von Kardorff and I. Steinke (eds), *A Companion to Qualitative Research*. London: Sage, pp. 58–62.

Flick, U. (1992) 'Triangulation revisited. Strategy of or alternative to validation of qualitative data', *Journal for the Theory of Social Behavior,* 22: 175–97.

Flick, U. (1994) 'Social representations and the social construction of everyday knowledge: theoretical and methodological queries', *Social Science Information,* 35(2): 179–97.

Flick, U. (1995) 'Social representations', in R. Harré, J. Smith and L. van Langenhove (eds), *Rethinking Psychology*. London: Sage, pp. 70–96.

Flick, U. (1996) *Psychologie des technisierten Alltags*. Opladen: Westdeutscher Verlag.

Flick, U. (ed.) (1998) *Psychology of the Social: Representations in Knowledge and Language*. Cambridge: Cambridge University Press.

Flick, U. (2000a) 'Episodic interviewing', in M. Bauer and G. Gaskell (eds), *Qualitative Researching with Text, Image and Sound: A Handbook*. London: Sage, pp. 75–92.

Flick, U. (2000b) 'Qualitative inquiries into social representations of health', *Journal of Health Psychology*, 5: 309–18.

Flick, U. (2004) 'Triangulation in qualitative research', in U. Flick, E. von Kardorff and I. Steinke (eds), *A Companion to Qualitative Research*. London: Sage, pp. 178–83.

Flick, U. (2005) 'Qualitative research in Germany and the US: state of the art, differences and developments', *FQS – Forum Qualitative Sozialforschung*, 6(3) (http://www.qualitative-research.net/fqs/fqs-e/inhalt3-05-e.htm).

Flick, U. (2006a) *An Introduction to Qualitative Research* (3rd edn). London: Sage.

Flick, U. (ed.) (2006b) *Qualitative Evaluationsforschung – Konzepte, Methoden, Anwendungen*. Reinbek: Rowohlt.

Flick, U. (2007) *Designing Qualitative Research* (Book 1 of *The SAGE Qualitative Research Kit*). London: Sage.

Flick, U., Fischer, C., Neuber, A., Walter, U. and Schwartz F.W. (2003) 'Health in the context of being old – representations held by health professionals', *Journal of Health Psychology*, 8(5): 539–56.

Flick, U., Kardorff, E. von and Steinke, I. (eds) (2004a) *A Companion to Qualitative Research*. London: Sage.

Flick, U., Kardorff, E. von and Steinke, I. (2004b) 'What is qualitative research – introduction and ovorviow', in U. Flick, E. von Kardorff and I. Steinke (eds), *A Companion to Qualitative Research*. London: Sage, pp. 3–12.

Flick, U. and Röhnsch, G. (2006) '"Ich vertrau' der anderen Person eigentlich …" – Armut und Obdachlosigkeit als Kontexte sexuellen Risiko- und Schutzverhaltens von Jugendlichen', *Zeitschrift für die Soziologie der Erziehung und Sozialisation*, 26(2): 171–87.

Flick, U. and Röhnsch, G. (2007) 'Idealisation and neglect: health concepts of homeless adolescents', *Journal of Health Psychology*, 12(5), in press.

Flick, U., Walter, U., Fischer, C., Neuber, A., and Schwartz, F.-W. (2004c) *Gesundheit als Leitidee? Gesundheitsvorstellungen von Ärzten und Pflegekräften*. Bern: Huber.

Gebauer, G., Alkemeyer, T., Boschert, B., Flick, U. and Schmidt, R. (2004). *Treue zum Stil*. Bielefeld: Transcript.

**147**

# References

Gibbs, G. (2007) *Analyzing Qualitative Data* (Book 6 of *The SAGE Qualitative Research Kit*). London: Sage.

Glaser, B.G. (1969) 'The constant comparative method of qualitative analysis', in G.J. McCall and J.L. Simmons (eds), *Issues in Participant Observation*. Reading, MA: Addison-Wesley.

Glaser, B.G. (1998). *Doing Grounded Theory: Issues and Discussions*. Mill Valley, CA: Sociology Press.

Glaser, B. and Strauss, A. (1965) 'Discovery of substantive theory: a basic strategy underlying qualitative research', *American Behavioral Scientist*, 8: 5–12.

Glaser, B.G. and Strauss, A.L. (1967) *The Discovery of Grounded Theory: Strategies for Qualitative Research*. New York: Aldine.

Goetz, J.P. and LeCompte, M.D. (1981) 'Ethnographic research and the problem of data reduction', *Anthropology and Education Quarterly*, 12: 51–70.

Goffman, E. (1974) *Frame Analysis: An Essay on the Organization of Experience*. New York: Harper & Row.

Goffman, E. (1989) 'On fieldwork' (transcribed and edited by Lyn H. Lofland). *Journal of Contemporary Ethnography*, 18: 123–32.

Green, J. and Thorogood, N. (2004) *Qualitative Methods for Health Research*. London: Sage.

Groeben, N. (1990) 'Subjective theories and the explanation of human action', in G.R. Semin and K.J. Gergen (eds), *Everyday Understanding: Social and Scientific Implications*. London: Sage, pp. 19–44.

Guba, E.G. and Lincoln Y.S. (1989) *Fourth Generation Evaluation*. Newbury Park, CA: Sage.

Guba, E.G. and Lincoln, Y.S. (2005) 'Paradigmatic controversies, contradictions, and emerging confluences', in N. Denzin and Y.S. Lincoln (eds), *Handbook of Qualitative Research* (3rd edn). Thousand Oaks, CA: Sage, pp. 191–215.

Guggenmoos-Holzmann, I., Bloomfield, K., Brenner, H. and Flick, U. (eds) (1995) *Quality of Life and Health: Concepts, Methods and Applications*. Oxford: Blackwell Science.

Hammersley, M. (1996) 'The relationship between qualitative and quantitative research: paradigm loyalty versus methodological eclecticism', in J.T.E. Richardson (ed.) *Handbook of Qualitative Research Methods for Psychology and the Social Sciences*. Leicester: BPS Books, pp. 159–74.

Hammersley, M. and Atkinson, P. (1983) *Ethnography: Principles in Practice*. London: Tavistock (2nd edn 1995, Routledge).

Hildenbrand, B. (1999) *Fallrekonstruktive Familienforschung – Anleitungen für die Praxis*. Opladen: Leske & Budrich.

Hirschauer, S. and Amann, K. (eds) (1997) *Die Befremdung der eigenen Kultur. Zur ethnographischen Herausforderung soziologischer Empirie*. Frankfurt a. M.: Suhrkamp.

Hopf, C. (1982) 'Norm und Interpretation', *Zeitschrift für Soziologie*, 11: 309–27.

Huberman, A.M. and Miles, M.B. (1998) 'Data management and analysis methods', in N. Denzin and Y.S. Lincoln (eds), *Collecting and Interpreting Qualitative Materials*. London: Sage, pp. 179–211.

Hurrelmann, K. and Albert, M. (eds) (2002) *Jugend 2002–14. Shell Jugendstudie*. Frankfurt a. M.: Fischer.

Jahoda, M. (1995) 'Jahoda, M., Lazarsfeld, P. & Zeisel, H.: Die Arbeitslosen von Marienthal', in U. Flick, E. von Kardorff, H. Keupp, L. von Rosenstiel and S. Wolff (eds), *Handbuch Qualitative Sozialforschung* (2nd edn). Munich: Psychologie Verlags Union, pp. 119–22.

Jahoda, M., Lazarsfeld, P.F. and Zeisel, H. (1933/1971) *Marienthal: The Sociology of an Unemployed Community*. Chicago: Aldine-Atherton.

Jessor, R., Colby, A. and Shweder, R.A. (eds) (1996) *Ethnography and Human Development*. Chicago: Chicago University Press.

Jick, T. (1983) 'Mixing qualitative and quantitative methods: triangulation in action', in J. von Maanen (ed.), *Qualitative Methodology*. London: Sage pp. 135–48.

Johnson, B. and Hunter, L.A. (2003) 'Data collection strategies in mixed methods resarch', in A. Tashakkori and C. Teddlie (eds), *Handbook of Mixed Methods in Social and Behavioral Research*. Thousand Oaks, CA: Sage, pp. 297–320.

Kamiske, G.F. and Brauer, J.P. (1995) *Qualitätsmanagement von A bis Z: Erläuterungen moderner Begriffe des Qualitätsmanagements* (2nd edn). Munich: Carl Hanser Verlag.

Kelle, H. (2001) 'Ethnographische Methoden und Probleme der Triangulation – Am Beispiel der Peer Culture Forschung bei Kindern', *Zeitschrift für Soziologie der Erziehung und Sozialisation*, 21: 192–208.

Kelle, U. and Erzberger, C. (2004) 'Quantitative and qualitative methods: no confrontation', in U. Flick, E. von Kardorff and I. Steinke (eds), *A Companion to Qualitative Research*. London: Sage, pp. 172–7.

Kirk, J.L. and Miller, M. (1986) *Reliability and Validity in Qualitative Research*. Beverly Hills, CA: Sage.

Kluge, S. (2001) 'Strategien zur Integration qualitativer und quantitativer Erhebungs- und Auswertungsverfahren. Ein methodischer und methodologischer Bericht aus dem Sonderforschungsbereich 186 "Statuspassagen und Risikolagen im Lebensverlauf", in S. Kluge and U. Kelle (eds), *Methodeninnovation in der Lebenslaufforschung. Integration qualitativer und quantitativer Verfahren in der Lebenslauf- und Biographieforschung*. Weinheim: Juventa, pp. 37–88.

Knoblauch, H. (2004) 'The future prospects of qualitative research', in U. Flick, E. von Kardorff and I. Steinke (eds), *A Companion to Qualitative Research*. London: Sage, pp. 354–8.

Knoblauch, H., Flick, U., and Maeder, C. (eds) (2005) 'The state of the art of qualitative research in Europe', special issue of *Forum Qualitative Sozialforschung – FQS*, 6(3) (http://www.qualitative-research.net/fqs/fqs-e/inhalt3-05-e.htm).

Köckeis-Stangl, E. (1982) 'Methoden der Sozialisationsforschung', in K. Hurrelmann and D. Ulich (eds), *Handbuch der Sozialisationsforschung*. Weinheim: Beltz, pp. 321–70.

Kowal, S. and O'Connell, D.C. (2004) 'Transcribing conversations', in U. Flick, E. von Kardorff and I. Steinke (eds), *A Companion to Qualitative Research*. London: Sage, pp. 248–52.

Kuckartz, U. (1995) 'Case-oriented quantification', in U. Kelle (ed.), *Computer-Aided Qualitative Data Analysis*. London: Sage, pp. 158–66.

Kushner, S. (2005) 'Qualitative control – a review of the framework for assessing qualitative evaluation', *Evaluation*, 11: 111–22.

Kvale, S. (2007) *Doing Interviews* (Book 2 of *The SAGE Qualitative Research Kit*). London: Sage.

Lamnek, S. (1988) *Qualitative Socialforschung (Vol. 1): Methodologies*. Munich: Psychologie Verlogs Union.

Lathor, P. (1993) 'Fortilo obsession: validity after post structuralism', *Sociological Quarterly*, 35: 673–93.

Lazarsfeld, P.F. (1960) 'Vorspruch zur neuen Auflage 1960', in M. Jahoda, P. Lazarsfeld and H. Zeisel, *Die Arbeitslosen von Marienthal*. Frankfurt a. M.: Suhrkamp, pp. 11–23.

Legewie, H. (1987) 'Interpretation und Validierung biographischer Interviews', in G. Jüttemann and H. Thomae (eds), *Biographie und Psychologie*. Berlin: Springer, pp.138–50.

Lincoln, Y.S. (2004) 'Norman Denzin', in U. Flick, E. von Kardorff and I. Steinke (eds), *A Companion to Qualitative Research*. London: Sage, pp. 53–7.

Lincoln, Y.S. (2005) 'Institutional review boards and methodological conservatism', in N. Denzin and Y.S. Lincoln (eds), *Handbook of Qualitative Research* (3rd edn). Thousand Oaks, CA: Sage, pp. 165–81.

# References

Lincoln, Y.S. and Guba, E.G. (1985) *Naturalistic Inquiry.* London: Sage.

Lüders, C. (1995) 'Von der Teilnehmenden Beobachtung zur ethnographischen Beschreibung – Ein Literaturbericht', in E. König and P. Zedler (eds), *Bilanz qualitativer Forschung,* Vol. 1. Weinheim: Deutscher Studienverlag, pp. 311–42.

Lüders, C. (2004a) 'The challenges of qualitative research', in U. Flick, E. von Kardorff and I. Steinke (eds), *A Companion to Qualitative Research.* London: Sage, pp. 359–64.

Lüders, C. (2004b) 'Field observation and ethnography', in U. Flick, E. von Kardorff and I. Steinke (eds), *A Companion to Qualitative Research.* London: Sage, pp. 222–30.

Lüders, C. (2006a) 'Qualitative Evaluationsforschung – Was heißt denn hier Forschung', in U. Flick (ed.), *Qualitative Evaluationsforschung – Konzepte, Methoden, Anwendungen.* Reinbek: Rowohlt, pp. 33–62.

Lüders, C. (2006b) 'Qualitative Daten als Grundlage der Politikberatung', in U. Flick (ed.), *Qualitative Evaluationsforschung – Konzepte, Methoden, Anwendungen.* Reinbek: Rowohlt, pp. 444–62.

Lüders, C. and Reichertz, J. (1986) 'Wissenschaftliche Praxis ist, wenn alles funktioniert und keiner weiß warum: Bemerkungen zur Entwicklung qualitativer Sozialforschung', *Sozialwissenschaftliche Literaturrundschau,* 12: 90–102.

Lunt, P. and Livingstone, S. (1996) 'Rethinking the focus group in media and communications research', *Journal of Communication,* 46: 79–98.

Madill, A., Jordan, A. and Shirley, C. (2000) 'Objectivity and reliability in qualitative analysis: realist, contextualist and radical constructionist epistemologies', *British Journal of Psychology,* 91: 1–20.

Mallinson, S. (2002) 'Listening to respondents: a qualitative assessment of the Short-Form 36 Health Status Questionnaire', *Social Science and Medicine,* 54: 11–21.

Marotzki, W. (1998) 'Ethnographische Verfahren in der Erziehungswissenschaftlichen Biographie Forschung', in G. Jüttemann and H. Thomae (eds), *Biographische Methoden in den Humanwissenschaften.* Weinheim: Beltz, pp. 44–59.

Miles, M.B. and Huberman, A.M. (1994) *Qualitative Data Analysis: A Sourcebook of New Methods* (2nd edn). Newbury Park, CA: Sage.

Mishler, E.G. (1986) 'The analysis of interview-narratives', in T.R. Sarbin (ed.), *Narrative Psychology.* New York: Praeger, pp. 233–55.

Mishler, E.G. (1990) 'Validation in inquiry-guided research: the role of exemplars in narrative studies', *Harvard Educational Review,* 60: 415–42.

Morgan, D. (1998) 'Practical strategies for combining qualitative and quantitative methods: application to health research', *Qualitative Health Research,* 8: 362–76.

Morgan, D.L. (1988) *Focus Groups as Qualitative Research.* Newbury Park, CA: Sage.

Morse, J.M. (1998) 'Designing funded qualitative research', in N. Denzin and Y.S. Lincoln (eds), *Strategies of Qualitative Research.* London: Sage, pp. 56–85.

Morse, J.M. (1999) 'Myth #93: Reliability and validity are not relevant for qualitative inquiry – Editorial', *Qualitative Health Research,* 9: 717–18

Morse, J.M. (2003) 'Principles of mixed methods and multimethod designs', in A. Tashakkori and C. Teddlie (eds), *Handbook of Mixed Methods in Social and Behavioral Research.* Thousand Oaks, CA: Sage, pp. 189–208.

Morse, J., Swanson, J.M. and Kunzel A.J. (eds) (2001) *The Nature of Qualitative Evidence.* Thousand Oaks, CA: Sage.

Moscovici, S. (1998) 'The history and actuality of social representations', in U. Flick (ed.), *The Psychology of the Social.* Cambridge: Cambridge University Press, pp. 209–47.

Neisser, U. (1981) 'John Dean's memory: a case study', *Cognition,* 9: 1–22.

NIH Office of Behavioral and Social Sciences Research of the National Institutes of Health (2001) *Qualitative Methods in Health Research – Opportunities and Considerations in Application and Review.* Bethesda, MD: National Institutes of Health.

Patton, M.Q. (1980) *Qualitative Evaluation and Research Methods.* London: Sage.

Patton, M.Q. (2002) *Qualitative Evaluation and Research Methods* (3rd edn). London: Sage.

Picot, S. and Willert, M. (2002) 'Politik per Klick? Internet und Engagement Jugendlicher – 20 Porträts', in K. Hurrelmann and M. Albert (eds) *Jugend 2002 – 14. Shell Jugendstudie.* Frankfurt a. M.: Fischer, pp. 221–68.

Polkinghorne, D. (1988) *Narrative Knowing and the Human Sciences.* Albany: State University of New York.

Rapley, T. (2007) *Doing Conversation, Discourse and Document Analysis* (Book 7 of *The SAGE Qualitative Research Kit*). London: Sage.

Reicher, S. (2000) 'Against methodolatry: some comments on Elliot, Fischer, and Rennie', *British Journal of Clinical Psychology,* 39: 11–26.

Reichertz, J. (1992) 'Beschreiben oder Zeigen: Über das Verfassen ethnographischer Berichte', *Soziale Welt,* 43: 331–50.

Reichertz, J. (2004) 'Objective hermeneutics and hermeneutic sociology of knowledge', in U. Flick, E. von Kardorff and I. Steinke (eds), *A Companion to Qualitative Research.* London: Sage, pp. 290–5.

Robinson, J.A. and Hawpe, L. (1986) 'Narrative thinking as a heuristic process', in T.R. Sarbin (ed.), *Narrative Psychology: The Storied Nature of Human Conduct.* New York: Praeger, pp. 111–84.

Robinson, W.S. (1951) 'The logical structure of analytic induction'. *American Sociological Review,* 16: 812–18.

Roller, E., Mathes, R. and Eckert, T. (1995) 'Hermeneutic-classificatory content analysis', in U. Kelle (ed.), *Computer-Aided Qualitative Data Analysis.* London: Sage, pp. 167–76.

Rosenthal, G. (2004) 'Biographical research', in C. Seale, G. Gobbo, J. Gubrium and D. Silverman (eds) *Qualitative Research Practice.* London: Sage, pp. 48–65.

Sandelowski, M. (2003) 'Tables or tableaux? The challenges of writing and reading mixed methods studies', in A. Tashakkori and C. Teddlie (eds), *Handbook of Mixed Methods in Social and Behavioral Research.* Thousand Oaks, CA: Sage, pp. 321–50.

Schönberger, C. and von. Kardorff, E. (2004) *Mit dem kranken Partner leben.* Opladen: Leske & Budrich.

Schütze, F. (1994) 'Ethnographie and sozialwissenschaftliche Methoden der Feldforschung', in N. Groddeck and M. Schmann (eds), *Modernisierung Sozialer Arbeit durch Methodenentwicklung und – reflexion.* Freiburg: Lambertus, pp. 189–288.

Seale, C. (1999) *The Quality of Qualitative Research.* London: Sage.

Shaw, I. (1999) *Qualitative Evaluation.* London: Sage.

Silverman, D. (1985) *Qualitative Methodology and Sociology.* Aldershot: Gower.

Smith, H.W. (1975) *Strategies for Social Research.* Englewood Cliffs, NJ: Prentice-Hall.

Spencer, L., Ritchie, J., Lewis, J. and Dillon, L. (2003) *Quality in Qualitative Evaluation: A Framework for Assessing Research Evidence.* London: National Centre for Social Research (www.natcen.ac.uk).

Spradley, J.P. (1979) *The Ethnographic Interview.* New York: Holt, Rinehart & Winston.

Spradley, J.P. (1980) *Participant Observation.* New York: Holt, Rinehart & Winston.

Steinke, I. (2004) 'Quality criteria in qualitative research', in U. Flick, E. von Kardorff and I. Steinke (eds), *A Companion to Qualitative Research.* London: Sage, pp. 184–90.

Strauss, A.L. (1987) *Qualitative Analysis for Social Scientists.* Cambridge: Cambridge University Press.

Strauss, A.L. and Corbin, J. (1998) *Basics of Qualitative Research* (2nd edn). London: Sage.

Strauss, A.L., Schatzman, L., Bucher, R., Ehrlich, D. and Sabshin, M., (1964) *Psychiatric Ideologies and Institutions.* New York: Free Press of Glencoe.

Strube, G. (1989) *Episodisches Wissen.* Arbeitspapiere der GMD (385), pp. 10–26.

# References

Tashakkori, A. and Teddlie, C. (eds.) (2003a) *Handbook of Mixed Methods in Social and Behavioral Research*. Thousand Oaks, CA: Sage.

Tashakkori, A. and Teddlie, C. (2003b) 'Major issues and controversies in the use of mixed methods in social and behavioral research', in A. Tashakkori and C. Teddlie (eds), *Handbook of Mixed Methods in Social and Behavioral Research*. Thousand Oaks, CA: Sage, pp. 3–50.

Tashakkori, A. and Teddlie, C. (2003c) 'The past and future of mixed methods research: from data triangulation to mixed model designs', in A. Tashakkori and C. Teddlie (eds), *Handbook of Mixed Methods in Social and Behavioral Research*. Thousand Oaks, CA: Sage, pp. 671–700.

Thomas, W.I. and Znaniecki, F. (1918–1920) *The Polish Peasant in Europe and America*, Vols 1–2. New York: Knopf.

Tulving, E. (1972) 'Episodic and semantic memory', in E. Tulving and W. Donaldson (eds), *Organization of Memory*. New York: Academic Press, pp. 381–403.

Walter, U., Flick, U., Fischer, C., Neuber, A. and Schwartz, F.-W. (2006) *Alter und Gesundheit. Subjektive Vorstellungen von Ärzten und Pflegekräften*. Opladen: VS-Verlag für Sozialwissenschaften.

Webb, E.J., Campbell, D.T., Schwartz, R.D. and Sechrest, L. (1966) *Unobtrusive Measures: Nonreactive Research in the Social Sciences*. Chicago: Rand McNally.

Wengraf, T. (2001) *Qualitative Research Interviewing: Biographic Narrative and Semi-Structured Methods*. London: Sage.

Westie, F.R. (1957) 'Towards closer relations between theory and research: a procedure and an example', *American Sociological Review*, 22: 149–54.

Willig, C. and Stainton-Rogers, W. (eds) (2007) *Handbook of Qualitative Research in Psychology*. London: Sage.

Wilson, T. (1981) 'Qualitative "versus" quantitative research', in M. Küchler, T.P. Wilson and D.H. Zimmerman (eds), *Integration von qualitativen und quantitativen Forschungsansätzen*. Mannheim: ZUMA, pp. 37–69.

Witzel, A. (2000, Jan.) 'The problem-centered interview', (27 paragraphs), *Forum Qualitative Sozialforschung/Forum: Qualitative Social Research* (online journal), 1(1). Available at: http://www.qualitative-research.net/fqs-texte/1-00/1-00witzel-e.htm; accessed 10 Sept, 2006.

Wolff, S. (2004) 'Ways into the field and their variants', in U. Flick, E. von Kardorff and I. Steinke (eds), *A Companion to Qualitative Research*. London: Sage, pp. 195–202.

Znaniecki, F. (1934) *The Method of Sociology*. New York: Farrar & Rinehart.

# Author index

# III Subject index